Karma Drama

Reincarnation and re-setting your Karma

Access past lives in Altered States of Consciousness, utilising such therapy as psychodrama.

Amazing past-life proven cases; part teaching manual

by

Dr Stuart R Rolls, PhD

Psycho-Spiritual Author, Therapist
and Teaching Practitioner

Learn my methods – you too can emulate

ALSO BY DR STUART R ROLLS, PHD

Self-help series:

Dreamology and Doctoring Your Dreams

Self-Help Psychotherapy

Meditating the Paranormal

Sensuous and Other Astral Experiences Now!

Self-help and autobiographical:

Afterlife: *My Amazing Two-way Contacts with* (in UK, NZ and Australia)

The Hereafter and Supernatural: *How YOU too can Paranormally Research the Afterlife, Past, Present, Future, 'Now-consciousness', Spiritual gifts, Transcendence and more*

East–West Paranormality: *Miracle experiences, yogins and adepts, psychics and spiritualists worldwide*

Fiction:

Getaway to Down Under – a steamy truth based novel with psychic undertones

Relaxation recordings:

Available online as CD or MP3 download
as backup to Dr Rolls' Self-Help series

DISCLAIMER

This series of books is advisory. Any health problems that could be affected by high tech. in meditational or dreamwork should be the responsibility of the individual; related choices should be made in consultation with one's own medical advisers.

NOTE

With regard to mention of cassette tapes in Dr Rolls' books, please note many of his recordings have been transferred to CD and MP3 and are available for purchase via the internet.

This is an IndieMosh book

brought to you by MoshPit Publishing
an imprint of Mosher's Business Support Pty Ltd

PO Box 147
Hazelbrook NSW 2779

indiemosh.com.au

Cataloguing-in-Publication entry is available from the National Library of Australia: http://catalogue.nla.gov.au/

Title:	Karma Drama: Reincarnation and re-setting your Karma
Author:	Rolls, Dr Stuart R
ISBNs:	978-1-925666-42-7 (paperback)
	978-1-925666-26-7 (ebook – epub)
	978-1-925666-27-4 (ebook – mobi)

Cover design and layout by Ally Mosher allymosher.com

Images from AdobeStock.com

CONTENTS

PROLOGUE

This book should captivate readers with its fascinating, reasoned and true accounts of our spirit survival after human passing. Also of our life after life reincarnations (not forgetting what our psychics can tell us for now). All's revealed in meditatively relaxed states. Finding the right practitioner or group is key; training in author's psycho-spiritual methods also revealed to them, within.

CHAPTER I

Updates on my psycho-spiritual experiences etc, completing book series

We all have our anxieties etc, maybe influenced from past life memory. Whilst completing my last book (*East–West Paranormality: Miracle experiences, yogins and adepts, psychics and spiritualists worldwide*), I drove myself crazy, thinking I would pass over and never finish it. Similar nervous feelings had come up in my life before but not to this shaky extent. Coincidentally (see on) I'd experienced, in Altered States of Consciousness (ASCs), past life access via therapy methods I've largely originated and refined myself.

Again, I realised I was picking up memory aspects of my past life writer-monk's life driven desperately (in previous books). He'd wanted to complete a set of language translations before he died. So much more knowledge of his 'Karma-Drama' (my term) was now harshly catching up with me, in this 21st century. Today we have evermore knowledge.

Cathartically, my anxiety is now clearing. *It has taught me first-hand, so much more on how I might help heal other's balance their karma.* This book (*Karma Drama*), is possibly the eighth and last of my mainly psycho-spiritual book series. A ninth book, entitled *Getaway to Down Under*, a largely truth-based rather hot novel, nevertheless had psychic under-tones of its own for readers, plus a measure of true psychological healing for its heroine and maybe some of my readers own selves, folks, therapists or groups.

Psycho-spiritual (encompassing general philosophical, psychological, spiritual leaning), plus now reincarnational knowledge, have been mounting themes of my writings. I interchange the classification titles and wordings sometimes for easier grassroots and professional familiarity and coming together understanding. However, I largely felt fated to write up the homely case for Spiritualism first, deeming myself lucky to be born into a psychic family, despite the knocks (all learning!), especially being wartime evacuated with younger brothers to watch over, for our loving, psychic Mom. I've had a rich grassroots psychic life, to be lucky enough to convey these things helpfully and as entertainingly as possible, from other aspects of my personality, various diplomas and university degree studies also.

Throughout all my books you will note a pattern building eventually of how to be fully applied researching the cause and effect of our Eternality and what it all implies. *It seems we are not born idly onto this or any other Planetary World*. I will do my best herein to examine the mysteries of karma, fate and rebirth, throughout my chapters. I shall be building on my other books and especially the last one, so inspired by going worldwide – 'East–West'. I researched the common conclusions shared by humankind, *no religion or group or place having the monopoly on our beautiful soul journeys* (if only we wish positively to make them so).

Every life's learning is only part of our whole and I'm hoping to now come up with new insights here, encouraged by contacts from my readers and 'guides'. This will round off my lifetime book series nicely but I might eventually come back free in another 'self', without monk's shakes (joking!).

Meanwhile, I'll briefly revisit some of my long life's 'case histories', as well as of family and others too, including clients', psycho-spiritually/parapsychologically but *with new karmic teaching depth.* These not so much now as in my fuller psychic accounts in previous books but more fully and capably evidencing their greater logical meaning into Eternity!

Long time readers will recall some of mine and others' recalled past lives in most of my books, e.g. *East–West Paranormality: Miracle experiences, yogins and adepts, psychics and spiritualists worldwide*:

Formally now, I make my earlier century ageing monk incarnation a chief teaching model. Additionally you might consider my incarnation around the Napoleonic period battles, though I seem to have been in two, a little confusingly. Anyway, my past life recordings of myself and many others overall, should teach so evidentially and with first hand proof.

Back to the monk: He was sequestered somewhere along an Adriatic coastline opposite Italy, frantically led to translating religious books from different sources. Keeping to our present book theme in a sense, it was as though I (as Hc) was reincarnating many old manuscripts too! Most were apparently from the many versions of Christian Biblical Latin; my job to render all into my then present Adriatic language and place.

He (the monk) would have known biblically about reincarnation, for wasn't there biblical reference to Jesus possibly being John the Baptist returned again to Earth?! Re other planets, myself as my old monk incarnation too (and others!) is obviously returned to Planet Earth now and not to some other Planet (a difficult concept which obviously I was unready for at the start of my earlier books). I felt desperate 'echoes' again, as stated, in present day Australia with the monk's past life fears washing over me again, that time might be oh! so desperately running out for me to finish a life's holy mission. His life and soul journey seemed threatened with incompleteness, the 'reaper' calling for him! Therefore, this life time around I've taken out insurance, bequeathing my works (including this one if un-finished, Heavens forbid!), safely to an inter-faith group to keep publishing, way beyond any of our present lives).

My tutelage and knowledge to pass on to readers, clients and cohorts, can be so enjoyed and emulated largely in altered state of consciousness – ASCs. I heavily took on the dying monk's anxiety, as main research model, out of my mind almost. Of course I'm still the same overall soul now, but hurrying still with cathartic traits release.

In a lonely cell (in that rare re-inheritance of previous incarnation) with a raw fresh-air space aperture – no window glass, high up one wall, I'd had a table loaded with many biblical books etc to translate. I had to paint illustrative pictures at the top corner of each chapter, showing what the disciples and their Master Jesus were doing; teaching and healing the sick for instance (much the same as in other Guru and disciple religions with Mastership conventions).

Slowed down by paints not drying quickly, and with several open books at a time cluttering my progress on my otherwise bare wooden table, I nearly gave up the ghost several times. Enormous stress was dealt upon me, higher by far than the stack of books waiting, or in progress. I just could not let my ailing self pass over before finishing my then vital work. I was overburdened with strain, anxiety and gathering weakness.

Similar stress was with me in my present life as I fought to finish *East–West Paranormality*. Definite key, karmic stirrings, of the old monk are still agitating me as I try get over them now (currently writing this *Karma Drama* end of series book).

Nowadays, I get up from my typing currently, doing a little of my yoga, plus tai chi stretching. This for staying fitter and meditative more in life now and to pacify myself from memory of the Holy Brothers strife. I've also been a semi athlete in this life, having once run track races, a 4 minute mile and 20 odd mile country runs. I built my own home too. In other words, I've learned 'balance' but I think I get that philosophy from a much loved Chinese guide.

After the above past life major recall, I shall come to further of self and near ones and clients re-calls, best underlining dramatically how past lives can leave us with hang-ups/neuroses etc, which make for excellent modern psycho-analytical healings. Some say more with Jungian Spiritual involvement. I have furthered this in my ASC and Karma/Drama research, healing and understanding, topping up my overall lifetime psycho-spiritual background. I do give much of the credit however to spirit guide's/guru's and often loved ones passed on, helping us more than we realise. The readiness to perceive is all, to paraphrase Shakespeare in Hamlet.

I predict that increasingly more as the years go by, with therapists (or one's self alone if trained appropriately; see later tuition chapters), our many past lives, healthily happy or unhappy, if examined, will make for Psycho-Soul balanced future lives. For instance, I personally can perceive now, that having endured and re-lived psycho-therapeutically, that monk's so desperate fight to translate for his cause, as above, he became somewhat martyred. I'm almost cured with that part of it mainly now, for 'both' our incarnations' sakes!! However, I still yet desperately fight and avoid taking up his painter illustrator art again in this life. Though a possibility, it's caused psychological compulsivity, I admit and can well do without (but am getting there)!

Here's an interesting point: Some of my grandchildren are quite good at art but granddaughter Larissa may have genetically picked up through my genes a deep propensity to stay in her room drawing and painting relentlessly and can hardly understand why. Her talents are great but must be draining and they travel with her wherever she lives. 'I don't know why,' she says. Readers, do make allowances for need to abstract present genetic influence from past life experience, per se.

Now over to other past lives' cases and references and spirit bi-location/transportation, more lengthily in the outstanding ones. Also over to my guide's once taking me in spirit to another planet, firstly with some preparation! Though for a reminder spot of humour first, Samuel Pepys the 16th century London diarist wrote in his then present life, words like – and re spirit transportation: Methinks last night I travelled from my chambers to my Lady Castlemaine's bed-chamber afar off, embracing her so closely, it was divinely true to my aching senses – I won't put quotation marks because I don't recall the very words, though the full meaning is there. How could I miss reporting a chance like that though?! I took similar astral travel, bi-locating myself once or twice, when sleeping away from home and beloveds too!

My first wife having died too young, I was not one for affairs and I had my first children to raise and set a good example to. Eventually however (and you'll read in this and my other books how karma brought me and my latter wife together, we having provenly been on Earth together before in France).

Again, you can go back in all my writings, noting that I didn't have any evidence of past lives with my first wife but oh! boy, the futuristic visions of her and a particular disability – also her far away home, were profound. Yet we were little children when I started astral travelling to her faraway home and school, bless her.

Years later also noted in my books, on the rare occasions when I was away from home where severe storms might be hitting (or was home in the same house but seeing to clients, unable to go down passages to the back of the house where the children and their storm-fearing Mum were), I could telepath comfort to her/them. At one time – it's miraculously worth repeating – my telepathic voice was tape recorded on a machine the kiddies were having fun with. This was two rooms and two corridors away, it being a large house. Such is known as Electronic Voice Phenomena (EVP), nowadays.

Science seems currently to be catching up with psychic phenomena generally. We surely must also give credit for my Guide's co-operative evidence brought about and offered through me.

Think for yourselves, dear readers and support scientific evidence that doesn't want to make cheap shots at the psycho-spiritual. Memorable data waits out there for all. Do value it's gathering proof. Go back and forth if you will, into my writings and evidence that even staggers me who's lived it personally and with my loved ones plus so many others. Seek again the psychic categories and as to what they mean.

These books have opened up so many of the following abbreviations etc:

- Clairvoyance, meaning psychic vision

- Clairaudience, meaning clear hearing (both from the French)

- Telepathy (akin to previous mind-to-mind transmission and reception, now consider it as above under EVP)

- Physical Mediumship, where entranced Mediums allow spirit friends, loved ones, teacher guides etc to speak through them – even materialise to sitters/clients.

Further, we have Astral Travel, generally to Earthly and Spiritual, not always heavenly planes, but note Swedenborg in my bibliography at books' endings; Spiritual healing can be via hands on energy in person, or directed via distant healing; Bilocation – one's spirit presence, seen in more than one place at once; even conversing with people who vividly remember such encounters.

Without preaching or favouring any religions particularly, there are mixed uses of the various spiritual/psychic gifts, also combined applications of the same 'gifts', all seen in the life of Saintly ones or as in Corinthians 2. 1, in the mission of Christ and his disciples/gurus and their student disciples etc, immemorable.

So! You see, I just neutrally hold the middle-ground in my psychic life to serve better. Being extremist invites fewer into the knowledge and blessings that one can so dearly pass on, in life/lives. Hence some of my book titles careful consideration (all with sub-titles): *East–West Paranormality* and this book's title *Karma Drama*, also *The Hereafter and Supernatural* etc. I won't go over the nine publications here but one subtitle, referred helpfully to *How You Too Can Research the Afterlife* plus there are many sound recordings of mine that can be found currently online as CDs and MP3s. However, I might find development and time to open a website soon. So far it's been years of a felt mission, all-consuming write, write, write! but so gratefully. I have my artistic granddaughter who I'm sure could think and draw up a funny cartoon for this.

Now on to my most favoured branch of therapy to help and entertain and teach you with …

CHAPTER II

More updates and deeper lessons; teaching emanating from them

Surprisingly, in this life's teens I took to all the yoga asanas without any instruction whatsoever. How and why? Standing on my head and doing all the yoga poses must have been practiced in a former life or two which I haven't yet re-visited. They could have come out of genetic or other memory causation I may later mention. Mental, physical, genetic etc?

Readers will understand why these questions had to largely await the closure of what unexpectedly became a deeply studied psycho-spiritual book series finale!

Regular readers will recall my other sworn lives where I've followed and been put down for faith in a particular religion (once at least as a Huguenot-Protestant in France). However, in other recalled past lives, in altered states of consciousness (ASC), I entertained at some Court or other. Also I was a young drifter put terrifyingly into stocks. Later I was myself a follower-practitioner of Anton Mesmer, father of Mesmerism (early hypnotism), with resultant ASC, and up to a point – maybe physical and early soul-healing, pre Freudian times!

In my practices in this life, relaxing energies have come through my psychic healing abilities combining with later voice-over relaxation techniques. I bow to Mesmer, Freud, Jung, Grof and all the pioneer Psychedelic Revolutionists and Transpersonal Psychologists increasingly leaning toward the spiritual, traceable back through all my writings. In *East–West Paranormality* I paid deep respect also, to founders of world faiths in general (may their followers increasingly become 'inter-faith'). However, never forgetting all good and kind humane world citizens, regardless of faiths, including then, all those still helpful souls gone on before. What of 'Space Citizens'?! Other inhabited Planets? We're not done with those yet! They must be 'out there'!

I've soul or karmically inherited a set of teacher/writer/ practitioner roles in this interesting life. Also, I was once an English Vicar, as told to me by a psychic in New Zealand. I recently sought out the Church of England's records, Oxford UK, substantiation for the 18th century records of this life, phoning their archives centre from 'down under' here in Australia. Karmic lessons again were derived, to advise my readership of, not forgetting those seemingly ordinary individuals who pass on their higher spirit knowledge sometimes and also on life in general. There are many spirit levels in the hereafter, and not the ones you can purchase at trades person's shops!!

Once again I had a past life spent in France, this time with a small vineyard, meeting again my sweetheart from other lives where we suffered as Huguenots. She and I in the last life before this life's togetherness, was where I ended up 'press-ganged' into a Napoleonic battle (I seem to be aware of having been in two battles, confusingly) but had that romantic 'sweetheart' involvement again as above; she looking only a little different but with fair hair once more (full details published for my readers in earlier books).

My 'sweetheart' and I met up again in this present life and she had the same past life remembrances as I did, laced with karma (broadly fate) we still hadn't come to terms with – and were destined be hit and hurt with yet again, if we weren't careful. Much is made of soul 'mates', so here was a prime example of such.

Return to my earlier books for the full stories of the above, but if you follow my teachings and self help book series, you will have amazing insights into what you are and have become through those, your very own past lives, believe me. I simply have to continue the privilege of advising on ASCs and practice, giving other practitioners guidance and teaching too.

No matter how good one's previous therapeutic careers, Multi-Life, Karmic-Healing Practice and Teaching etc, ought ideally be experienced, and prepared for Professionally before practicing personally.

In Psychodrama type group and individual practice and training, (which I will return to throughout this book) we spend a huge amount of training for sufficient expertise and Directorship Qualifications. All helps makes us modest, as you'll note throughout the chapters. We largely get cured first of our own hang-up's which could get in the way of helping others.

I claim world-first authorship of my chosen *Karma Drama*, avante garde and descriptive pioneer wordage with acknowledgements primarily to Eternal Spirit, the very real pioneer! Plus I now add 'Soul Drama', with all its connotations of ASCs.

Re past lives: I do acknowledge Psychodrama and other therapies for helping my colleagues and I through this life's immediate hang-up's first. I also thank Eternal Spirit for my 'school of hard knocks' experiences etc, over several known lifetimes, blessing me that I may pass on this progress for humankind.

Throughout this book I will show you how to reach the ASCs etc which helped the individuals and groups of mine into their own self knowledge. 'Know Thyself' as the Greeks of old would have inscribed over their temples, positively and with 'soul many lives' inclusiveness no doubt. Not repeating the same past-life mistakes but learning from them, more humanely and with growing spirituality, such as will lead to better lives here and hereafter.

You don't have to be religious to follow me or anyone. As Britain's Winston Churchill would say, "Give us the tools and we will finish the job" (this for Roosevelt's American help in the last World War).

So! Having raced through my last book, facing up to being awfully haunted by past life memories of my life as a dying monk, wishing only to complete his works and mission, I've made it! I'm still existent, on Earth here, materially! Or, back again for another look around before other planetary or finally spirit-state only lives and experiences! Where indeed will it all end, but we are all as old as eternal existence; in the everlasting non other than that which the continuous 'now' presence advocates, surely?

Yet another thing, however, might have been haunting me lately and prophetically. I'm just getting over several gruelling admissions to several hospitals.

I've been enabled to have just starting writing again – one of my two beautiful daughters spending three weeks from England helping me convalesce, my other darling near me in Australia keeping an eye on me too. I was fortunate also to have my beloved son collect and comfort me here and transport me miles to his more suitable hospital at dead of night, in desperate pain.

I'm back! Again there's no stopping my great desire to pass on the beautiful truths I've been permitted to share, as part of my mission in life. There will be more reminders of past lives, prophecies, healings, miracles to relate -many family ones too, one might say, with both my dear sons, also dear daughters as above. Our lives, as in my various books, were 'magical', spread around England, New Zealand and Australia, and the magic is still ongoing.

Finally, my books, ebooks, meditational recordings (CDs and MP3s), are all available online. Just use my name and title to look them up at your favourite retailer.

I am as indicated, over the dreaded, shall I say monk's complex of fears that he 'wouldn't make it'!? I'm getting so relaxed now. Healed, just about, from that past. Years of Psychotherapy per se couldn't have done this for me. It needed what I'm concentrating on in this book, namely *Karma Drama* (my personal copyright term, sub and main title, chiefly utilising ASCs).

Please do safely learn, enjoy, heal, teach (see on for more instructions), from wheresoever or whatsoever you are coming from. You can work in couples, groups, or even individually, with safeguards. The series and following chapters reveal all.

Practitioners do realise, amongst my many roles, psycho-spiritually, I am a Psychodrama director. My next venture directing, may be in group film making, if I can make it, though I'm so unbelievably reaching peace now, after my 'past monk life' re-visitation. Peace no doubt stirring cathartically from me after other 'Past-life Re-visitation' and 'Psycho-Spiritual Healing Revelation' too. Writing again about this has been so cathartic; 'Soul Drama' and 'Soul-Karmic' Freeing. I truly want similar blessings for all my readers.

Peace and Blessings to All – in following teachings from mine – an extraordinary lifetime's current experiences – not all Earthly but with Spirit inspired contact and thinking. A few of my past-lives' remembrances, and more of others, in group or working alone, included herein too. Thus you will find much of my terminology unusual, some kindly say 'original', 'avante garde' and refer to it variously as 'comforting, relaxing, free, neutral, refreshing, non-prejudicial to any cause or other beliefs, not scary at all but fascinating'.

My early boyhood education was held up by the last World War. My first book shows more my grassroots everyday and spiritual learning, thanks to pioneer Spiritualism. Very many years later an Open University system and the advent of Parapsychology started up and added to my hopefully overall wisdom. I was a married man, largely self taught, with then three lovely children.

However, just as 'my monk' would have been learned, I'd been learned and a practitioner etc in several previous lives (see on). Life and lives are the true educators. Caringly, I pass their wisdoms on to All, (including readers, family, friends, fellow humans, educators, practitioners and their clients etc, as and if appropriate).

CHAPTER III

More stories/accounts re-assessed, especially space-trip Out of Body Experiences (OOBEs); Remote Viewing (RV)

Space-age visitation to habitable planets for us may be years off yet. Discovering material 'beings 'out there', to inter-communicate with may take infinitely longer Actually probing more with our psychic and spiritual insights, as with Indian swamis like Bhaktivedanta Swami Prabhupada, may make soul voyaging (SV), remote viewing (RV), bi-location (B/L), more popular and evidential. This with other books than just *Easy Journey to Other Planets*, etc (see bibliography).

Indian religions in general well cover our possible inter-planetary lives as well as astral/spirit ones. Planetary questions enquire why are we bodily/physically born and purposed into this, just about only inhabited planet (Earth) we know of. So varied is it in it details, features and co-ordinates etc. (It has current world atmosphere, hemispheres, continents, countries, counties, towns, villages, houses, names and numbers, varieties etc, etc, – a one-off only evolution). Collectively we might prefer to think of it as unique, impossibly nothing like at any other 'place' and/or time, wherever and whatever, in endless Eternity. How little we know!

Statistics may make the above would be rash equation look incomplete. Before my books end we may conclude there is no beginning or end to habitats, life or lives, material or spiritual.

Therefore Earth may have countless clones! T.S. Elliot wrote similarly on this point, "In my beginning is my end" (but I'm jumping the gun a bit here (see later more spiritually/philosophically concluding chapters).

However and conceivably, other planetary lives we might have had would surely have affected our eternal souls but in ways inexplicable to our present sense consciousness. The same might be the case for other planetary beings. I've had very little bi-locational experience of other planets (see on), so can only make slight assumptions personally. Perhaps we get so heavily soul-immersed here, we can only recall recent familiar type lives on Planet Earth. Also what's customary to us now, locks us into our own projections as to what other planets and planetary beings might be like (they experiencing likewise). Yet all the answers are apparent somewhere in the eternal 'now of Eternity'.

Though human life reputedly started in Africa, long centuries ago, Africans initially could have but little idea of what physical lands might be beyond them, let alone outer space ones. Luck and chance would have influenced matters there. They weren't ready to imagine, like us today, other space beings, vaguely like themselves maybe, could exist beyond their global reaches. More advanced today, we can surmise that grander civilisations and constructions are 'out there'. We project the familiar and 'the readiness is all', say our bards.

It might be stretching a point here but relatively, regions in space and their vibes must surely connect with ours soon – the converse no doubt being true. Could we be the only ones to have started a venturing rocket age? Analogously, our individual life styles and behaviour from early Africa to more modern advancement East–West (some said 'never the twain shall meet'), caught up fully and eventually, beyond their long unexplored, unnatural, Earthly demarcations! Though humans were admittedly of the same Darwinian gene pool.

Once we're here on Earth, past-life researchers in the paranormal literature, like Dr Ian Stevenson in cases of reincarnation, will go to any place on Earth and re-find you, no matter where your Earthly past lives were.

I've re-experienced a few of my past lives as readers will have noted. One outstanding one especially with my recent wife Sheila. Other psychics told me about more previous lives we'd shared, though self evidential ones are more convincing. In our present lives we separately undertook ASCs (altered states of consciousness) 'trips', detailing separate re-calls of our last relationship on Earth together. Would-be Practitioners please up-skill and work out the ramifications of your cases with clients, when able. Note e.g., I was killed in a Napoleonic battle. Sheila lived on to meet and be with someone else and I wasn't alive at that time to know about it. So therefore it could never have been in my past life memories, only Sheila's. That's why we mustn't assume too much in any analysis. Incidentally I believe that 'someone else' turned up again in this century! Well! We don't have be with the same souls forever!

Recorded past life incidents of self, groups, others, clients etc – and relative scenario's above, are in my writings overall. Sufficient to help all; (individuals, friends, practitioners, society at large). If I need to repeat them and other experiences of psychic nature again, in the context of this series end of my books, it will bring them refreshingly and more meaningfully up to date completely.

Before I remind my long term readers about my own little planetary trip let me say I don't always do things alone and certainly not without help from beloved 'guides' or 'gurus' as in spiritualism and yoga/the psychic or psychical generally – psychism is a rarer term. All such aspects were referred to and made more familiar in my previous books, especially *East–West Paranormality*.

Ingo Swann, I recall, was the 'other' referred to above, a science oriented writer, known as a pioneer in 'remote viewing'. I became aware of him and remote viewing as such, a lifetime ago in England (see my earlier books therefore). He reputedly was able to 'visit' other planets and bring back knowledge of their chemical compositions. I don't know how he managed this and decades might pass before his 'present outer space' knowledge might be proven. However, I noted recently in an old *Mysterious Universe* computer article 'NASA Discovers Organic Matter on Dwarf Planet Ceres'.

The Skeptics Dictionary quotes 'Remote Viewing' (RV) is a fancy name for telepathy or clairvoyance etc, the alleged psychic ability to perceive places, persons, and actions that are not within the range of the senses'. Governments use it in espionage etc. I'll come back to the psychic faculties terminology but what of my own (?), one time only, (dwarf) planet experience, from author to you, dear readers, faithfully sworn to be absolutely true!

Firstly folks, let me joke. I used to work in Psychiatric Institutes once, so I know something about the mind and nerves! No! I'm not unbalanced or mentally poorly!

Readers will know enough of my life and psychic mother and grandmother beginnings now, plus a sadly missed, passed on brother, who re-appeared to me and saved me from a cold death, alone on an icy park lake, aged 8 or 9. I'd already been seeing clairvoyantly or with 'remote viewing' in school class, visions of my future wife, her country cottage, school etc and yet I'd never left our English Midlands Big City and home (physically!).

Soon the second World war would be upon us. The electric lights would go out. Mother would sit her little boys around the fire glow. It had a crystal-ball effect upon her and she'd relate prophecy that invariably came magically true, often within days. Throughout my life too (in this potted though psychically and spiritually blessed history here), I would foresee folk and events in mine and my family's future, plus develop more spiritual gifts, psychic healing included, as I grew more compassionate.

Always I was aware of spirits from other ages and cultures, helping and teaching me the spiritual gifts that the 'Skeptics Dictionary' attempts to categorise dubiously, though not too unkindly. If readers care to look, they'll find that I categorised in my last book, op cit, psycho/spiritual cases from my own sworn heartfelt truthful experiences (no bias).

My books are crammed with such as the above, not to make show but to learn, teach and practice psycho-spiritually. Under my category of 'astral travel', I will end this chapter on its planetary theme (and why not other planets, broadly, as future homes for our eternal spirits!?). However, it will help you, I feel, to think of my travel in the spirit to distant Earth locations first '(One small step for Mankind', Neil Armstrong said but his 'magical', historical, moon trip, was physical).

Astronauts have lots of preparation and simulated practice for space walks. I think my guides, over years, prepared me for my own 'Journey to Distant Planets' as well as to my own heartfelt Earthlife's latest mission reincarnationally, to write and prove psychic matters. Also they have further guided me, I'm sure, into earthly practitioner use of sound-relaxing, plus psychological techniques and care. I'm usually aware psychically and spiritually when guides or guardian angels are watching and caring over me/us; passed-over loved ones and friends too, whether during normal sleep, in relaxing meditation, or much the same – ASCs, depending on their depth. However, we all have our own spirits, to co-operate with all as above or not, regardless.

However, various spirits' energy and ways (unseen but mostly experienced as caringly supporting me), would nevertheless do seemingly crazy things with the 'real me' spiritually'! It was as though I was accompanied and shown, in spirit, habitats like lake beds, just sitting there in clear daylit water, picking up and feeling as well as seeing the intricate shapes of shells. It was beautiful down there. Then I'd be just as peacefully be taken back to my resting body, to gently let it come to physically and take in the seeming psychic miracles.

I must add that I'm not a good swimmer and hardly like to get out of my depth normally and especially after nearly drowning in childhood at that lake, where my late brother's spirit appeared to point me in a safe direction, off the ominously cracking ice.

So! Sitting beneath that later lake surface at peace, knowingly comforted by my guides as on so many previous occasions, after that earlier frozen lake mishap, what next? Firstly a word about that reassurance. It's more than any ordinary, comforting, reassuring, safe feeling, that one is not alone. A bit like when ones had a bad dream but a loving parent comes to comfort. Or when a warm hearted teacher reaches out to a child bullied by masters at a previous school, as in my case. Repeat, 'what next'?

My kind teacher hero, with poor bent back, reached out to

me when another had flogged me when I was barely aged ten. Being psychic himself, he recognised me as psychic also. He always praised my writing and prophesied, more than inferred, that I would be authoring spiritual books one day. Wow! I was then so introvert and junior.

In the psychic career preparations I've alluded to I was drawn to spiritual/psychic healing. Some call it distant healing, or healing in the Spirit, or absent healing where one is miles away or separate from the 'healee'. The healee is the someone being in need and receipt of yours and your guides help, the basis of a lot of prayerful and faith type healing vibes East–West – global outreach wherever, regardless of particular faiths or movements.

Many accounts are in my book 'series' of my spiritual healing per se, a lot of it at a distance but it has been mainly present touch, gentle hands-on energy, in person. It can prolong lives as in the case of my first dear wife (earlier books mainly).

My spiritual guides increasingly took me on astral travels to bring healing to some 'clients' (I never charged them). Amazingly I would spiritually zoom over landscapes to recipients in need. They would sometimes see or sense my living spirit with them. Not all of my spiritual healer colleagues in England and elsewhere have passed on yet. I've been unable to get to one with my own recent illnesses, though I've been so very busy with the book series and past-life monk energy legacy.

Those readers that aspire to all aspects of healing in general, do note the places you pass over or arrive at. This for convincing proof later. I noted peoples home descriptions, furniture etc, anything out of the ordinary, even though I'd no knowledge of them or their part of the country or world. All I would have would be letters for help in answer to my healing at a distance adverts, addresses more or less superfluous when one is' flying blind'! My adverts address would get such wonderful detailed thankyou's in return, proving what I'd witnessed and done.

If all this sounds incredulous to the critical may they try my techniques (much to follow, further chapters) and open mindedly read mine and others' psychic experiences. I might add that when still fully practicing I had groups up to Sydney from our Australian Capital City, Canberra, including Medical Doctors, Mental health workers, Politicians, Scholars, Folk from all walks of life, all profoundly moved and grateful for their experiences with me (not forgetting my spirit helpers cooperation with me, of course).

Tomorrow I will get around to my 'space trip and slight landing' but I've been typing and reviewing all day, in between an author's background research and hard checks, study and inspiration, so I'm exhausted. See you in the morning friends! Tell your friends and folks about mine and other's lifetimes etc spent wishing to guide humankind, with psycho-spiritual real truth they can lovingly share. This perhaps initially, in that our loved ones etc, gone on before, really can respond to you and all if sought by your own love and powers, or another's, if more gifted or practiced.

I may say more later about mischievous, earthbound or lost spirits but honestly I've never been bothered by them and if anything have helped them. They're 'Lost in Space' (remember the TV series?) so to speak (often our space). So dubbed spiritual church/meeting place 'rescue groups' exist to help them.

My books have related already many of my astral travels to spirit world regions and to astral planes in between, linking with our loved one's gone on before, also contact with wonderful guides and helpers in general. Any notion of being totally separate from all of this is mistaken. It's akin to seeming like the separation between us and humans who one day may have sufficiently conquered space enough to live 'out there'. The point here is that we can never in spirit be totally cut off on Earth or anywhere. Again we can refer to 'Lost in Space' similarities. Yet in the afterlife, or Eternity (even in hellish low places, lostness – in this case of soul, can be re-educated and commuted). See e.g., Swedenborg's *Heaven and Hell*. Let's all send love and light amongst that gloom and doom stuff.

Stepping stones for my dwarf planet visit, were earthbound training trips in my soul, around, Kent, UK, where I'd once lived. These, I remind, were for reaching out in my spirit to sick folks writing for healing at a distance, often with the flimsiest of addresses whereby we might keep in 'normal contact'. I began by supercharging my healing thoughts successfully (best in the sleepy evenings) for locally sick ones, family and friends, on familiar territory. I could hardly believe my success rate. I'll detail a main one, quoted in my earlier writings but again so worthily because it had a fun ending:

A lady in question but from way North and in no way on familiar territory, wrote that she was suffering from absolutely agonising skin eruptions (hives?). Also, that she was driven to desperation. This moved me, so I settled in an armchair upstairs, held the healing request letter, concentrated and settled down, lights out!

Not much longer after that I felt my usual trance-like feelings come over me and a floating off at easy but quick speed. Soon I was aware of a light coloured house in the moonlight, single storey and I got down to earth effortlessly -as if safely lowered down (as usual by another power), guide's obviously. I took in the single building, its smart, obvious front door steps etc and its overall size. Soon I was inside that front door gazing around, without any volition effort from me, simply looking around in the moonlight within. It had lit up a light oak furniture suite but the wardrobe was too big for the alcove by it. I then began to feel like an intruder and was directed to look through an open doorway where I could see a double bed but held my hands out quickly in front of me to transmit healing energy and then leave.

The above I later conveyed to the 'healee' and she wrote back to the effect that she'd been miraculously healed and for me not to return, otherwise her husband would think she was having an affair!!! She also acknowledged that the bedroom set in question had to be returned because the wardrobe wouldn't fit its intended alcove!

My faithful guides collected me again another night but this time it seemed on a longer trip. I had no idea it would be so far but at 'soul speed'. They, the guides, I trust implicitly at 'the controls' with me, for they know I'm happy to let them teach me always, as it's all destined to be written down for you and posterity!

Anyway, this was the space trip I'd saved for chapter ending, I descended (aware I was not alone but was, as customary, with spirit guardians). Lowered down this rare time, much as on my earthly astral travels but seemingly this time on another planet. It appeared small, different, seemingly temperate, with cloud reflections and sky formations of (I try hard to think back accurately) greens, pink and yellow? Then I was aware of the curve of this heavenly body, less than moon size, I figured. I stepped back (in my spirit of course) because It felt alarming to see the horizon dip away so. I thought I stood on some patchy, light scrub, lichen or other greenish to light-brownish shades of growth, on a pumice like flat base. I didn't think about breathing or an atmosphere. It's unnecessary in the spirit. Perhaps this is what guardians had prepared me for in the lake. The whole but short amazing trip was overwhelming. I wished afterwards I'd turned around to see if there were any rising landscapes. After that my faith in after-life/angelic helpers ever increased. For now they've brought me more down to Earth for our writing legacy. So be it!

CHAPTER IV

Altered States of Consciousness reveal us in past, also present lives with their evidence on bi-location

We all can astral travel without prior knowledge of the much varied spiritual gifts, see St Paul in the Christian Bible Corinthians 1. 12, plus others East–West. I mentioned further in *East–West Paranormality* that it pays to diligently take note of as much detail you can whilst 'out there'. Otherwise, it's like opening up, say, Tutankhamun's tomb and closing it without examining all the wondrous contents. I've already mentioned remote viewing (RV) but this is generally regarded as viewed from stationary position, not astral travelling or bi-locating as such, the terms intermingle).

As already stated, this book will almost certainly be the last of my unintended nine psycho-spiritual books series (it importantly being also a teaching manual). Another psychic medium 'impossibly' predicted spirit would use my mind like a typewriter in helping produce them. I give again here credit to souls 'on the other side' for helping predict and dictate them. Wow! All comes to me through of course my psychic abilities. Repeat, they've run into the nine separate, in their own right, book titles, that without intention from me became a series.

One of my books was more a 'steamy' novel I confess but truth based – *Getaway to Down Under: London to Sydney, Australia*. Also it had psychic truth and prophecies laced into it. Overall in my writings, words and messages would flow to me, déjà vu-like, which had to put down at speed sometimes before they were lost forever. Inspirational or Spirit Inspired Writing it's been known as. There's certainly no Berlin or Mexican Wall between us and our Spirit fellows!

Back to astral travel and bi-location subject/s: (they intermingle remember), I've been influenced by my guides to go over this/them again with new emphasis on the fact that we in Australia today and elsewhere, can now do today in spirit – 'magically'/parapsychologically, what saintly spirits of earlier century faiths could do. Milarepa of Tibet for instance or the Buddha, actually born near the Himalayan foothills (see *East–West Paranormality*).

1. Well I certainly doubled up on both healing and astral travel, bi-locating from Australia here, when I Iay down late one afternoon years ago, concentrating healing for my first dear Mother in law, ill in hospital, overseas and skies in UK. I'll return below to this, because I need to check how international time fitted.

2. Also (readers will recall) whilst on a bus to a lecture at Sydney University, I fell asleep. My astral body (you have yours too!), whilst the bus was still way off in transit, my spirit some way ahead, was seen by my colleagues in Psychodrama. One, a senior nurse greeted me way back of Sydney Uni', outside a lecture room soon to be utilised for a Stanislav Grof's mighty Transpersonal Psychology Teach-in. As a stranger, I had looked at the uni brass plate, entered the grounds and followed all the arrow sign directions marked for Stanislav, to the appropriate lecture hall. "George is just inside waiting for you", called out Mary, the nurse, training in psychodrama too.

George was indeed looking out for me and we had a chat,

being both in training for Psychodrama Directorship, he being a drug and alcohol Counsellor cum Psychodramatist and me – as I like to call myself – being a Spiritual Psychologist or Therapist. Or, Parapsychologist and Psychic.

Suddenly, in my consciousness, a voice was urgently calling out elsewhere, "Here's your stop mate, wake up, quick". I thanked him hurriedly, for I'd told him earlier I'd never been to the uni. Exactly as above, everything happened all over again, only this time in my physical body! Mary and George were left so speechless. I myself could hardly believe what had truly happened.

Back to 'Mother' (my Mum in law), from no. 1/ above (the page, not Heaven!!). I'd quoted 'late afternoon', but was it so? It must have been almost 40 years ago, because my girls Faye and Jennie (known from my books) were at their Australian junior village school then. In spirit I 'visited' 'Mother', before Faye and Jennie arrived home.

It takes but moments for my minder guides to propel me through space across the world spiritually (as 'in the spirit' – spirituality having wider connotations as in say holy matters and being). Of course, when I took off (not even in the air for that's not a spiritual component!!) It must have been early dawn in UK. My spirit awareness and my physical memory being obviously still with me, hovered over a city unknown to me but noticeably with spires and grand stone buildings of a lovely hue.

I descended slowly not by my own will but under my spirit guardians easy control. All I had to do was 'go with the flow', similarly as I am doing partly now with them inspiring my writing. All credit to our teacher guides and yes they, bless them, they too have healing and so many different roles also. It's not so unlike having teachers, helpers, trainers, guides and guardians on Earth.

Anyway, by now I was being drawn to a smart stone building, the double doors with big ornate brass handles. I felt blocked, unable to enter there. I was 'floated over' to a smaller, similar building then and through its brass handled doors, embarrassed because painters had sheets down, whist they were doing a colour scheme – two-tone walls with a black divider strip. They never noticed spirit me being gently controlled, safely and astonishingly, through yet another, but single-handled door to the middle of a ward. Why such an ornate place and doors for a hospital!?

With my normal reserve, and thinking other patients and staff might notice me stood there, I nevertheless noticed 'Mother' at the end bed on my right. She sat up, obviously seeing me and crying out. Energy zoomed through me and an 'inner voice' instructed me to quickly point my (spirit) hands in healing mode toward her.

Almost immediately it felt, I was back in Australia, the girls home on their own, late from school! They'd had a long, late walk home, not having been picked up by me, Daddy, as usual. They were calling me and asking why I'd left them long worried, but so glad to hear I'd 'been in England with their poorly Nannie'. Yes! The timing internationally was right but a few minutes earlier and the healing would have failed. I would have been physically awoken by the girls before 'mission accomplished'!

Later my Bro-in law contacted to say the churchy brass handled doors were once of Catholic Nun usage and the painting plus colours were exactly as I'd witnessed. His Mum was soon protesting as to why I'd been dismissed and she herself was soon dismissed from hospital (after previously having, with her bad heart, coughed up blood). She gained more happy life and we – family, returned to all in England awhile later, as my readers would know. The city, of beautiful stone work, it transpired, was Northampton.

These accounts and more raised topically throughout the book (some repeats), are not simply psychic story accounts as in my earlier tellings. They are meant also to now be deciphered years on with my later wisdom hopefully, as to what they prove for you and Humankind. I've examined major religions and what of the spiritual meanings behind them and all come up with similar findings, some more explicitly.

Assuredly we have karmic interplay, spiritual after-lives and many new lives, until we move on to something greater and blessed but that's for later chapters. Meanwhile, woven into my overall book fabric, some of my proven stories/cases, are selected as teaching ones for would be practitioners. As my medical/therapy oriented friends advise, my pioneering work is very avant-garde, examined for its deeper meanings as well as fascination, from my lifetime's deep, privileged experiences. However, I never forget the grassroots homely experience that Spiritualism gave me, nor our passed-on loved ones that communicate still, nor the many fine mediums, amateur or professional that link us.

I was just about ready for the next chapter here when the phone rang, disturbing my flow. I usually take it off the hook and answer calls when I take a break. I'd been seeing a friend Dr John England, my cardiologist, receiving a good report and he was now ringing. He'd shown a poet, who was also his client, a copy of *East–West Paranormality*. I ascertained if John had been reading the book (he'd loaned it to the poet). 'Yes indeed,' he replied, 'and I will have it back. It's wonderful; it's out there'!

The feedback was so warming but I'd met Dr John in other circumstances. We connected with another doctor who'd taken a therapeutic interest in Vietnam Veterans, suffering post traumatic war stress. Although we had various psychological and medical degrees and diploma's, we all had an interest in Psychodrama, here in New South Wales some years back (notably in the Blue Mountains), Australia. I still take part continuing more as a writer and researcher, having had children to raise after the premature death of my first wife (another relationship and more beloved children to provide for later but I'm happy in my writing career for All). Time has moved on. Eternity never will! (see on and on!!!)

CHAPTER V

Author's psychic healing adaption in hypnosis, mesmerism and karmic exploration states

Again I remind this is the possible last of my eventual nine books that unintentionally ran into a series. Each is complete in its own right and title but with additional learning, insight and practicing over the years (whilst raising two families). A wealth of knowledge that helps complete the fabric of this my maybe final range-covering 'Psycho-Spiritual Spectrum' work.

Also, you see, that previous monk-life of mine still holds some -but gradually lessening karmic sway over me. This in my 'karma-drama' fear of passing over yet again, before a life's mission seems finished. I might have more to write on this in my Conclusions, after main chapters. Especially so, having faced up to the problem therapeutically, in this my beloved, ongoing psycho-spiritual writing career, practice and life.

Back to karma and it's admixture no doubt of lesser sounding sub influences like accident/s fate, destiny, chance, societal shaping and learning, even genetic inheritance and vaguely instincts. Readers, do sense out your own shaping toward your present self, as I have, variously as a monk, vicar, writer, translator, Napoleonic Wars 'press-ganged' soldier, vagrant, harlequin and more unfathomed yet (though not inter-planetary yet as far as I know!). Sitters or group members of mine may be satisfied with 'tripping' to less past lives than I have but some of mine were researches for my books.

You, to be alive now, as you currently exist, will have gone through lots of similar and different past lives. Instincts can often tell us things about our many lives aspects without actual past-life research. ASCs may come up with bits of our current life memory aspects however; memories that may ring true but be images of movies once viewed etc. Therefore we mustn't get too carried away attributing too much in our imaginations, though really, lots of past life recall is so utterly intense, real and provable, as to absolutely deny mere imagination.

Just off the top of my head, I recall a very senior male Psychiatrist in one of my groups who's secret was that he'd lifelong been irrationally terrified of childbirth somehow! He could not keep still in my group and seemed to be writhing in deep fear, pain and distress. Afterwards he explained he'd intellectualised this horror as having being due to an Aunt of his who suffered direly in childbirth. At lunchtime he abruptly deserted the group. When asked why, he poured out cathartically that it had been 'him' in a previous incarnation, lying 'suffering' there that day. He added then that he was rushing home to give his wife a baby at last, and make amends for his earlier tragic refusals!!

Psychics sometimes tune in to our previous lives past. 'Soul Mates' from past lives assuredly do meet up again on Earth, way beyond co-incidentally. Read mine and wife Sheila's case in this and elsewhere in the series, I swear by! Also, about my first wife Barbara Rose, whom I knew about from detailed visions when I was a little boy. Sadly she died young but still appears to me and wanted me to marry again, finding another sweet Mum for our children.

Dreams, symbolically will throw us maybe, though if psychologically analysed, tell us not so much about our other lives but what present life state they've brought us to. In other words, to what we are in the very present here and now karmically. Some folk seem to have positive spirit contact during sleep.

Barbara's foster grandmother called me out of my dreamstate one night; she'd recently passed, and kept calling out her surname Booles – then unknown to me. My daughter Faith only recently told me she was frightened of possibly 'seeing spirits', so now I'm careful to add see 'in visions or on astral planes'. These things become so natural to psychic seeing, that we don't always stop and think what we are saying. We should realise that others may fear we mean seeing full-on with ordinary, everyday sight instead of our psychic gifts.

The Christian Bible advises somewhere for us to be sure the spirits are of God. Without being too sacrilegious I try to be of open multi-faith, East–West, so let me simply say, certainly there are silly spirits that can kid us with nonsense but guides and gurus worldwide protect us from them in our earnest research endeavours. (I'll point out the mischievous etc; see on.)

Lucid Dreaming institute's, associated article writers and practitioners, do utilise differently oriented ASCs (altered states of consciousness), some which might loosely lead to past-life enquiry or fancy or enjoyable dream like fantasy. ASCs ('getting into the zone'/'mind set'/specialised concentration or similar) are utilised too by sports folk etc.

Gerry, a friend and neighbour who presented me with a recommendation for *East–West Paranormality* is now more open to altered states. He'd written re his technical career and mainly logical left brain thinking, that my clairvoyance for him at another friend's mini party had surprised him and was the real deal. Later I'd try and telepath single mindedness for him in his bowls hobby and he now truly uses his mind in left brain/right brain balance, winning performances.

So! We can all develop our minds psycho-spiritually. That's not to say to being psychic per se but that left brain/right brain balancing creativity, can take us wherever our cold logic left brains once operated almost alone. Additionally though, re broad mind/mystical co-ordination areas, where we once believed maybe only gifted others could operate; may all join their ranks. 'Altered States' open the soul door! There are potential geniuses, saints and admixtures within all of us! Stand by humanity for a better, more spiritual world!

My book series show all aspects of the above and more, not forgetting creating back-up relaxation recordings my readers can obtain too, all available online. I might return to more of the above before book's end. We've barely reached the halfway stage yet.

So! I examine my own depths and ponder for my reader, my own whys and wherefores as examples. I've been so busy writing and researching to see yet if I've had opposite sex past lives, sensing assuredly that we all would find that we truly have. Lives too where we've slipped back or advanced by following the mores of our many incarnations. Soul memory discomfort or it's opposite offers experience to build upon, or dissatisfaction enough to work at any slipping back feeling. These things no matter how great or small, continue our 'schooling'. Indeed the 'schoolroom of life' is a very good metaphor for all our souls' progress.

Mesmerism, but later century known as Hypnosis predominantly, might be used for humorous fun and entertainment, at which most of us laugh. However though, readers please do wait until you've read chapters VI and VII and you'll realise the mind must not be treated carelessly. Don't worry, I'll see you through, but this last book of the series is being aimed at all the wonderful therapists out there, as well as the clinician within you all. In home relaxations (chapter IX), many of you careful readers might try to safely learn about ASCs for yourselves (again I'll be giving guidance).

To many of us, ASCs come quite spontaneously. Others apart from us might say, 'Oh! He or she is an old soul'. Often they can independently sense the identities of previous lives lived and recorded in our souls, Such was Biblically said and written by Christ's disciples about him being John the Baptist re-born again. The disciples however, were trained in the psychic and spiritual arts by Jesus. St Paul well covers these in Corinthians Chapter I. Verse 12.

In *East–West Paranormality* I truly gathered evidence worldwide for matching or similar spirit knowledge, beliefs, communication etc (with their cultural differences and histories of course). Of all the world's minor and major religions/belief systems, no one has a monopoly. All of us humans ask about where we come from; where we might be going to, and related questions. Worldwide, despite our religions etc, we usually expect a life hereafter and sense that it can't be the end of everything.

I conjecture about Universal/Planetary beings and their possible spiritual beliefs and practices too; if and where local 'mortal stages' have been met and reached yet, but so logically and in endless space surely? If so, these would be advancing along some sort of evolutionary continuum, that's also surely logical?

Back now, as here and throughout the book generally, I must keep referring to actual evidential accounts, supporting our past, present and future lives beliefs. The way I practice relaxing clients and counselling them generally in their present life problems, is with much the same technique and adjustments, as with any needed for past lives (see on).

Anyway, returning to the backbone cases in the book we research and re-examine for their greater meanings, was a young lass in Auckland, New Zealand. Her parents had brought her to see me (and this is a good case out of many life-long); I was only told that she had suddenly lost her voice and no hospital GP or specialist could help. Many of my 'healees' would have given anything for successes, but I had a day job and felt any grateful reward was in my having spiritual healer guides. I'd only allow clients to allow mere expenses for advertising, plus suitable home practice and rooms.

The lass laid down on my 'relaxa' couch quietly as I placed a cosy cover up to her shoulders. I'd heard about her loss of voice from the parents in the waiting room – nothing to go no really. Speaking to the maybe eleven year old in a gentle, father-ly way, she nodded assent to my laying a comforting hand on her forehead and dimming the light. She became nicely relaxed. I talked to her gently about remembering times before she had lost her voice (readers will note again that similar vibes that I use to physically heal folk, also helps them relax via hand on forehead other treatments, namely past lives research, psycho-logical healing too, memory as in the above blessed case).

Thank goodness she could hear. As she could not speak I took her, step by step in her acquiesive mind, to the times after, then the actual day in which she lost her voice. 'Now picture what happened I said firmly, don't let it stop your voice any longer'. She shuddered. A few more encouragements and suddenly she let out an almighty scream. Her parents rushed in as she was so clearly back in voice, she explaining volubly what had happened to her. The alarmed but so happy parents hugging her as I turned up the light

The lass apparently had taken the family baby out in their pram for a walk. On the return journey she'd had trouble with getting it down a kerb as she tried to hurry with baby and pram across a hilly road. Her grip on the handles let go. She screamed and froze then, thinking it would run away downhill into an oncoming truck. Fatefully the pram did run off at a slight downhill tangent but stopped at the opposite kerb. The dear girl somehow safely rescued baby and pram, making it home – herself mute and traumatised.

Now, wait for it. Here's more. I've just revealed to you (above) my 'secret energy' power adaption, which I initially stumbled upon in my hands – simply willing comfort for my sick, beloved first wife Barbara (as parents do with babies). After coming 'down under' I certainly used it without thinking to help the little Kiwi (New Zealand) lass. Also everyday clients to relax thereafter and of course dear second wife Sheila. Practitioners do not have to think that they must have this special power adapted into their work, but I've been so blessed to have received it into mine, to relax even the most impossible and resistant of clients.

All is in my earlier books, but as was my understanding and growth then, years ago. Any recall here gives the reader profoundly more updated understanding and analysis than first recounting 'but wait, there's more', as TV advertisers eagerly proclaim!

Well! Back in the proverbial 'then', I'd experienced Spiritual or as equally known, Psychic healing, researching in London, with a Saint on Earth, Harry Hitt (who worked in a factory by day, washing bottles). Evenings used to find us travelling in his poor old car, to visit the sick who couldn't get to his healing meetings. He used to urge me to put compassion and my love into my hands so as to aid his healing mission for the sick. He'd also urge shy young me to think kindly of their loved one passed on. In both cases, crippled and hurting folk felt betterment, also contact evidence from me of their beloved Heavenly ones. (Bless you forever dear Harry, a genuine soul and my Guru indeed!).

My dear first wife Barbara had had rheumatic fever as a child, affecting her mitral heart valve. We were only in our early twenties. Harry had predicted details of my return to my own city Birmingham, UK, where I would meet her, my first girl friend. She and I were prophesied to meet (by Harry but by my boyhood visions and astral travel/bi-locations too-full story earlier books). She'd get so breathless with mitral heart valve affected by rheumatic fever as a child. I'd be so compassionately moved as to place healing hands over her heart, thanks to Harry's 'love in your hands' instruction. All this recall saddens me but I must pass on how we can all learn to open up our psyches for others. Practitioners, please note again and learn. These 'miracle' teachings cannot be repeated often enough for you.

So there it is. My secret is out! I discovered too, by and by, that gentle hands on and willing energy to Barbara's forehead would soothe her over the years, when unwell. I then progressed to use the same overall energy in separate applications, as shown now, in general Spiritual healing, and more psycho-spiritual ASC research but still forms of healing work. More will be revealed as we proceed to other chapters. Not forgetting Psychotherapy and Analysis/Psychic reading, and Hypnotism/

Mesmerism and Soul therapy overall. It's been a busy life, believe me.

Not being conceited, I never really saw myself as a regular psychic healer but one's real working faith progression, as such, can dawn on one. Let's see ahead what other new light is revealed under the healing, psycho-spiritual banner.

CHAPTER VI

The use of psychodrama-type therapies etc., in addressing karmic influences

Joseph L. Moreno and his wife Zerka figured greatly in Psychodrama, Joseph having written quite a heavy primer on it, entitled *Who Shall Survive?* Zerka came from America to be present at Australian workshops I attended (see on).

I don't wish to engulf readers in heavy academic theory which they can look up privately at their ease; see bibliography. Let my teaching style, personal evidence and warm accounts, as kindly shared in by my sitters and others, take over. Practical experience examples are the best teacher overall, don't you think? I'm not writing a one subject treatise but covering so much of the whole psycho-spiritual-spectrum. Some aspects may stand out more than others, in the books series best looked at as a whole.

Readers might ponder at this stage what everyday human contact and challenge have to do with their karma, past and after-lives, the psychic and the spiritual? Historically, humans had limited contact, self-knowledge and gurus to guide them. In human therapies such as Psychodrama and now my very own, so personally christened 'Karma-Drama', past and after-life re-experience and psycho-spiritual awareness of and growth, can be streamlined into everyday practice. I've spent a long lifetime getting here for you and pray for everyone's spiritual growth and success!

Repeat, the Greeks of old inscribed on their temples for us to 'Know Ourselves' The above paragraph truly shows how in modernity we can do this. Now back to the pioneer Morenos:

When Zerka Moreno (now widowed) came 'down under' she gave us brilliant lectures and insight. She helped us deal with somewhat of a megalomaniac group member. He would always show off, grovel on the floor, shove anyone away after getting them to feel sorry for him, become the centre of attraction and if he had any role played, it was in the final analysis, seemingly, himself as some 'Almighty'!

The above is unusual and the group dealt with it under Zerka's guidance to 'mirror' himself back to himself (terms like that do come up in the practice, as well as modelling etc). Previously members had found it hard not to show their contempt and/or hit back at the 'almighty' personality above, but group hostility and anger is catching. All would realise by degrees and with a good director in charge, that 'we are all on the pathway of error'. (I referred to this earlier as 'trial and error learning'.)

Now was the above reflecting past life stuff? This single gent in question was normally bright, balanced, courteous, and held a responsible job. However, this was the eighties and I hadn't researched past lives at that stage and become a group director.

Although psychics can sometimes see into people's former lives, this is not commonplace. This might have helped me personally whilst self induced 'tripping' – the term being from the psychedelic revolution era. I didn't use or need drugs fortunately. I'd long practiced East–West meditation, Yoga techniques, especially energy breathing, Tai Chi latterly and always drug-free safe entrance into ASCs.

Coming back from England to make a new start back in Australia (again the eighties), re-acquaintance was first with my family branch in Perth, West Australia. Also, I met up with Dr Max Clayton, Psychodramatist but also Uniting Church Minister (not that one had to be a Churchgoer). He showed me around his Psychodrama Workshop. It had a stage. Being then more reserved in nature I baulked a little at acting out (role play) one's 'stuff' there, somewhat on show possibly.

Sadly, I never did enrol for Perth groups, by later moving onto Sydney, NSW. I'd lived there previously and thought it might give me more chance of furthering a psychology career with my new found English degrees etc. This chance had stopped more or less when I'd left Psychiatric nursing as a younger man, not enough in wages for the little family I was proudly raising.

Dr Clayton had arranged workshops in NSW, where we met up again later and I began training with him -hundreds of hours yet to come. Max moved on eventually but had helped my training-hours along, part of which was about my 'stuff', 'hangups' or 'withholds' if you like! 'Withholds' having come from my brief experiences with Scientology, not to follow but to add to my professional education.

Sydney workshops were continued by Dr Bill Spence. We'd sit in our group circles and first chat away generally until certain current, past or universal -whatever issues, might arise. These would touch on life to the point that an issue would stand out, if not several. If too many and/or too clouded, Bill would get the sitters involved to stand in the groups middle and state their 'stuff' whether troubled, pained whatever (there could be so many hurts and issues at the start of a whole weekend workshop, that amicable sort-out was necessary). The rest of the group would be invited to choose, then stand supportively behind the group member, who's case they felt closest to and needing of help and expression.

Generally speaking, over mainly weekend workshops but others more lengthy, issues would narrow down with all group members having every chance to present and deal with dissatisfactions out of their own lives. One could feel too conspicuous at first but soon fall into and be inspired by the group energy, learning by others individual cases,

Several 'in' words crop up in Psychodrama and I'll just use them as they crop up. A client stepping into a circle would be a Protagonist. They would be coaxed perhaps to walk around and arouse or feel their stuff. It might be say a woman who's obviously moved and the Director observing her body language might ask why are you shaking, or what are your clenched fists or stiff arms saying. Maybe embarrassed, she'd loosen up and try to look at ease. The group too might begin to then urge her to open up, the Director allowing and encouraging where necessary. Eventually the now so encouraged woman would say something like 'It's my bullying old mother in law, coming from the old Country; I don't mean to be disrespectful but I'm a young grandmother myself and she's a, a …' The woman starts crying and blurts out, 'I have to put up with her alone for two whole weeks and my poor husband, her son, died. He was terrified of her anyway.'

The offending mother-in-law, as above, would be known as the Antagonist. The Director might say, 'Choose a group member to play the part of your bullying old in-law now'. She chooses a reactive-looking other female for this (but fortunately one anxious by then with her own stuff). Director again to protagonist: 'Imagine your home now in all its detail with your in-law arriving' (this action in psychodrama is called Concretising the scene). The young gran in her own right, describes the scene and contents, then staggers in through an imaginary doorway (her own of course, 'concretised' in 'Surplus reality'). She starts ranting at the volunteer stand in. What continues to happen then is role-play, and role training, the couple being Director-guided to reverse roles over and over again until results are positively clear.

Do look up psychodrama and allied therapies for yourselves dear readers as complete coverage here would take a book on its own. I have to keep an entertaining flow.

Above, the young gran protagonist had found the strength in group support and its directorship to eventually inform her antagonist mom-in-law that she had to stop ranting or go home immediately, that it wasn't her (the young gran) who'd made her son emigrate but his mother herself, always bitter at her own husband's walking out on her. Also, she'd been bitter about young gran (protagonist) marrying her son.

To cut matters short here let me say here that in role play enactment the group's first chosen member arrived at scenes with group encouragement where she shouted back at the antagonist repeatedly; decades of bullied fear and holding back evaporating.

Tears and sorrows had flooded out for young and older gran enactments and role reversals. Refreshments and hot bath offered and run (in surplus reality exercise of course) and much 'pretend' catching up, peacefully then. Great acting, but it all worked out on the day.

Old gran on eventual arrival at the Aussie home, became so happy to be welcomed by her daughter (eventually too, her in-law's grown offspring and their children, some so welcomely looking like her passed over Son). The psychodrama ongoing legacy had uplifted the whole family and helped them put the past behind them.

I think the above shows Psychodrama in action, rather than my having dropped a whole lot of heavy theory on readers. I will no doubt come up with other cases or uses in the book writings continuance. Good examples are welcome in any subjects by and large. Since Chapter five regarding Mesmerism and Hypnosis but more to emphasise adding 'spiritual gifts' aiding their inducement, (I've since found in the literature something about the conjunction of ordinary Hypnosis and Psychodrama. I'll perhaps refer again to this in my chapters, no doubt.

At one workshop, Dr Bill Spence noted me sitting with hands under my thighs. 'What are you sitting on your hands for Stu?' he enquired. This was body language I had no idea I was exhibiting. Such 'language' speaks for itself really, how one looks taught and stiffened somewhere, looks, ill at ease, nervy, uncomfortable, to be putting on 'airs and graces' or whatever. There is a whole gamut of things one sees, feels, or might like to mention, that has indicators. Director then probes as gently as the situation allows or as the feeling seems right. (Readers do emulate these skills, especially if helping reassure clients in homing in with their past lives under your supervision and care. As in most things, 'practice makes perfect'.)

Different practitioners/therapists and fascinated but careful others, may choose to bring in aspects of their own training and expertise (as in the conjunction of Hypnosis and Psychodrama above).

Returning to Dr Bill Spence, he got me to stand and walk around the circle, concentrating on why I'd unconsciously allowed myself to 'sit on my hands'. I tried to reason that being rather new to Psychodrama, I was just feeling uncomfortable. That wasn't good enough for Bill, who was also a Psychiatrist. He kept reassuring me to not so much relax, for that is counter-productive in some cases. He incited the group to help me open up too. I felt mixed emotions until someone called out very perceptively 'and you're still keeping your hands back'. That did it! I felt I was back as a child. Mother whom I dearly loved was remonstrating at me. The flashback that came over me found me wanting to hit out at her.

Shock, horror! Please don't jump to any conclusion regarding the above. How could I possibly hurt my Mom?! Let me explain. I'd been the middle son of seven (no sisters) these were poor times in England. Always I ran errands for my dear Mom and from the age of four! I'd help with the babies – anything! Mind you, one poor older third brother, Bruce, had died and the eldest, Alan, lived with grandparents, to be located near his grammar school. The second son had become a rebel, with quite a gang in the street; he was never around to help but would be up to mischief (family and peer group position influences children's psychological growth so much). So! I was left the next oldest to help dear Mom, though I don't think I could ever have hurt her deliberately (yet had a memory of an extreme situation, being hit first by Mother – that's life!).

Above I mentioned how I did a lot of the family shopping starting as a mere four year old. This brings me briefly to cover Genetic Memory. Mother's parents kept laundry receiving offices, hardware shops and ran insurance rounds etc, naturally knowing how to wholesale as well as retail. It all came naturally – genetically – to four year old little Stuart me! Granted Mother would wrap up the necessary money within an 'items to purchase' list; if not enough money, instructing me to use my own discretion; also not stop and talk to anyone. I obeyed diligently (pre-school age recall!). If e.g., no ham for Father's then work sandwiches, or not enough money, I would arrange cheaper sandwich fillings. If worker Dad's pay had about reached weekly run-out point (he was an ex-soldier adjusting to civilian career), I would bargain! I'd say e.g., 'then give me some bacon or other left over bits off the machine please'; then, e.g., again, 'Dad will be hungry on the night shift, can you spare us some of your broken biscuits as well please?'

I guess, so young then (and having very curly hair until school start), I appealed to shop assistants. They would often serve me last (and offer a chocolate biscuit for myself – yum, yum), so no one else could question my being favoured; one young male assistant would knowingly wink at me. Thanks be to Genetics, I'm sure, they found in me a business like nipper; in the vein of his maternal grandparents!

Tailpiece: As a married family man in between studies in later life, I and my own little family took up several shops and small businesses, between UK, NZ and Australia. Again genetically driven, as above, I feel sure! (Another factor in assessing past life v genetic memory.)

My own psychic learning/teaching and especially writing, seen as a duty and mission to pass on, was also evident early on, forecast by a kind, male teacher – a psychic himself, when I was but ten. I've written in autobiographical form, here and there in the series, for anyone to relate to things as genetic, or identified with as potentially past-lives material.

Mother once used the words upliftingly, 'Stuart can do anything'. They became, I think, a non-conceited mantra-support for me by the time I got through infant to junior school.

I then was meeting with cruel male teachers, sometimes war victims of post traumatic stress disorder (PTSD), their pupils having to suffer with them. One could not hit back at canes and blackboard rulers without ending up in Borstal so-called institutes.

Psychiatric institutes which I myself nursed in as a young student in earlier days, were also places used too conveniently for the merely disobedient, broadly non-compliant and generally misunderstood. Psychology and in all its new branches, has so moved on since, thank heavens!

I repeat, the dilemma for my sat upon hands and psyche remained for many years until I took up psychodrama. How could I hit back at one so sweet but needy as my Mum? My memory in the matter was, I'd partially recalled, something about her tensing to hit me – her little protector! I don't think I ever sought any special privilege but she'd never done this before and I probably felt wronged, cast out, ungratefully treated in the moment. Also ashamed that I could lift my little fists to one so dear; a mother who gave her all to her family. Who knows what therapies or further stage Karma Drama can lift, free or advance for you/us!

There are other branches of Psychotherapy and methods of course, including Fritz Perles' Gestalt therapy, examining and treating clients mind/mental structures totally as in their present, complete, overall state. It opposes breaking them down into parts separately, treating behaviour (Behaviourism) symptoms of underlying Psychopathology) as a whole. In short, using one frontal attack seemingly.

The above Gestalt method, in my experience, would not be as successful as mainstream Behaviourism in any Psycho-dramatic Soul-karmic healing growth.

So! Unless I find room or more reason to give time to other than what you now see as my favourite truly tried and tested methods, I'll pass on now to refining our own safeguards in wonderful 'trips'. Join in the magic more settled now, full knowing I and my guides have largely pioneered all for you. However, do look to the bibliography at the end of the book or where I hope to find and mention one or two others somewhere along the same path. There may be occasion for extra mention of Lucid Dreaming, 'Eternal Now' authors Etc, the Monroe Institute, also the Synchronicity organisation, mainly USA-based and all of who's studies I've worked not too dissimilarly with, and grown psycho-spiritually more with, in different aspects.

I remind readers again, as in my book series as a whole that Master Charles of Synchronicity, Virginia USA, once said to me with a grin, 'I know nothing about spirits'. Even so He's tops and so erudite with his relaxation sessions and onward training toward blissful altered states of consciousness. He certainly advanced the art with me, as with the Monroe Institute USA too, not forgetting the Lucidity Institute, also of USA, and others worldwide no doubt. Yoga techniques are somewhat different with their physical as well as spiritual training, which certainly helped me along life's way. Psychodrama brought me directorship qualification.

The above take you so far, with their own particular bents brilliantly, some as to how the individual (in some instances) may easily float away their 'stuff'! Collectively, and with good old grassroots Spiritualism and Psychic Research, I built on all of these kindly disciplines and came up with Karma Drama and group therapy ways to more harness this.

Now let's look at being cautionary with nevertheless still

ground-breaking Mesmerism (adapted into modern day hypnosis). Also, let's be aware of any looseness with side-tracking the results of any of the above paragraphs splendid movements or other aspects. Over!

CHAPTER VII

Taking care not to short circuit mind and 'trips', thus better and healthier accuracy

Sharing a holiday camp holiday with two of my brothers years ago we attended a hypnosis late evening show at midnight. So late indeed that we felt sleepy with the relaxed music being played. Exactly as the hypnotist would have wanted. He arrived late. This might have been a psychological ploy to get the audience anxious or extra tired, therefore willing the showman to hurry and reveal himself and work.

On arrival the 'showman' hypnotist spoke as calmly as the background music, subjects not slow at co-operating after the tiring delay. After getting the whole audience to place their hands on top of their heads with fingers locked together, 'growing tighter and tighter until you cannot free them and desire me to magically help you', he continued. One can imagine the rest. He followed up with inviting those whose hands would not unlock to come up on stage, the rest of the audience to sit down and for everyone to enjoy the fun.

Many holiday campers would still be somewhat tipsy and so open to suggestion at the end of their fun day already. Great subjects for the hypnotist to exploit entertainingly, e.g., boo-hooing as if they'd lost their Mommy or maybe dropped their ice-cream cornet on the beach -whatever! But did the showman have enough savvy to bring them back skilfully from what we might refer to again as 'make-believe-surplus-reality', similar to

Psychodrama, previous chapter? We'll bring in Karma Drama below.

We're beginning to see similarities in any sort of mind changing – even entertainment-based. For instance if subjects are made scared in any way or told to act and believe that they're more stupid than they really are – under hypnosis of course, such beliefs may long prevail, unless properly freed, like the hands on head.

Karma Drama, currently new upon the scene, with my teaching and usage of 'Psychic Energy Altered States', relaxes clients/sitters/groups (or one's self personally into what they personally experience in their own 'trips' see earlier Chapter).

No hypnosis or 'slips' from anyone. Only gentle therapist encouragement for relaxation (usually with 'sacred' type music also helping all observe things for themselves). Just gentle holding one back from sleep, reassuring, caring, non-intrusive; lightly administering therapist at your side, helpfully assuring one be free of any past life difficulty blocks, ideally understanding how to integrate all into present balance.

More detail on Karma Drama with two chapters yet to come plus a final Conclusions chapter. Back now to my early days away from my native city of Birmingham. I think I was still early psych' hospital training, still in my early twenties.

I saved up hard to afford a popular British Therapy Association, Hypno-therapist's appointment at his London address. My first visit to our capital. I was that keen and early. I got there before he was breakfasted almost. I had a frustrated anger suppression problem – well sort of and who doesn't! I was driven in my past lives also I suppose, to be stronger, not give way all the time, and research what I'm now doing at last in this life – helping in the overall human psycho-spiritual field.

The Therapist invited me in. He turned out to be very wise and kind. A little questioning of me, then he pronounced that yes, he could hypnotise me the way I wanted, to stand up to a bully of this lifetime (well young life at the time!). Also get over thrashings from male bully teachers -mentioned earlier chapters; one in particular at a boarding school quadrangle roll-call head count. As a house captain I had to tell him who was missing and why. He accused me of covering for boys who weren't present, screaming 'liar' at me after I told him one was home on compassionate grounds and the other was in sick-bay.I replied 'I am not a liar Sir.' He locked me in a small room for Sunday church suits storage and marched the boys off to supper. He soon came back from the dining hall and beat me up, I being seventeen then and strong enough to punch back but daren't.

Allowing all the above had left me cowed and subdued I nevertheless felt ashamed I'd innocently put up with all of it. The hypnotherapist understood that I wanted him to sub-consciously direct me to overcome my withholding and truly thrash back at such brutes. He refused my request but not without explanation that the suggestion would short circuit my natural instincts from safely worked out caution. He wished me well and I gratefully felt that after his decision I'd cope better and not feel lessened (as with later past-life stuff, I knew nothing of then). I felt I could now work things out for myself and without a mental prop or crutch, that would have robbed my developing selfhood. Most of the pupils acted warily when the 'sicko' – as they privately called him – was on duty.

Thank God for that enlightened man, who wouldn't charge me. Readers do see, all these therapies in question, link up overall. I wouldn't be what I am today without that surely spiritually inclined therapist, a lifetime away. I could still have been quavering inside instead of ignoring others' sick aggressions.

As you've read, I'm so much more in touch with my past lives nowadays, especially the Vicar who had the temerity to question misguided (only) church authority, and the monk who wanted to translate what he saw as his days truths. I was able too, after that Napoleon war's past life session, to be more philosophical about it, and the folly of war with so much more human wrong activity. All brought to more understanding and desire to help clients and readers of mine, in my now Karma/Drama etc teaching role.

The chapter heading lists care in hypnosis, 'subliminals' and also 'trips', 'generally for better and healthier accuracy'. Yes! We must indeed watch what subjects put into our minds that short circuit sometimes our own judgement. We might for instance have subliminal advertising inserts played just below the threshold of pleasant music. It could register subconsciously with us as we go up and down the isles in whatever market or other place we may visit (the subconscious takes more in than we think). We might thereby also be lulled into purchasing things we don't want or need.

Such is some of the sales pitch above for entrepreneurs and companies to sell us recorded courses in mind, soul, sporting or any development. It can be virtual hypnotic programming for say sporting or any other activity. That's okay if honourably made clear and acceptable to us, as in most things in life.

'Brainwashing' is everywhere, respectful, parenting, teaching etc fine, but readers let me say again, do be careful of all suggestion based stuff, as in that hypnotic, often infantalising holiday entertainment wrote of further back. Okay of course if you don't mind. A general rule is let your minds be controlled in life only with directions you wish. This of course is different in past-lives research where only you can view their events or dramas though the session director or aides are helping you get the best out of what you reveal.

Several modern Institutes (as with traditionally Eastern Guru/disciple relationships) attempt to simply but beautifully teach us true meditation. This wherein we can reach altered states of meditational consciousness, peace and ecstasy.

One such Institution is The Monroe Institute, another The Synchronicity Foundation, both of the USA. Firstly, way back I took a tape recorded postal course with the Monroe Institute, wishing I could have visited it personally. But years later met up with Synchronicities founder Master Charles who set up another base in Melbourne Australia. (See below, also bibliography).

The Monroe tapes had been very informative and relaxing but taught me to watch for slip ups in my own work. Yet they described wonderfully how its founder went 'astral flying' (my brother Doug' once told me he had experienced this too. Mine have taken me places also, as in this book series).

I mentioned 'slip-ups' above. I felt one such as I listened to the gentlemanly, erudite Monroe tape, suggesting I think, that as we tuned in and entered sleepy or altered state, it would be as easy as rolling off a log into water. I'd nearly drowned as a child in that icy lake recall (see back) and reminders weren't helpful. Also as a child I'd seen at the cinema how logs were transported down rivers from forests at a higher elevation. Lumberjacks would sometimes have to clear log-jams by jumping upon them and poking them free. I'd get nightmares that they would fall in between them and get squashed!

With Master Charles (once Brother Charles but promoted

by his followers), I felt the same as I did about the scholarly Monroe Institute founder presentations. These were brilliant guys bringing multi thousand years old Eastern philosophies, meditation, relaxation, altered-states skills, more technically to the West.

For me however, I was disappointed when Master Charles told me with a half-spooked grin, he knew nothing about spirits. I went on then to make my own tapes (now reproduced and available as CDs and MP3s, as mentioned previously).

Once my Karma Drama, end of series book is under publication, I might then consider having my own website and/or change to niche publishers, but we'll see.

Naturally as a psychic myself, the above emphasis and profoundly further dimension will be in my works, it being so special to be able to keep in touch with our loved ones in spirit, gone on ahead.

Readers will know by now that I'm very careful to keep all positive and non-spooky with my teachings and practicing over the years. Years in which I've held free groups in my homes often, for love of service and the rewards of exciting inter-earth contact with spirit state worlds everlasting. Why think space travel amongst physical worlds will be non-spooky and sometimes scary when we come up against the end of our known faculties and understanding. Suffice it to say that scientific research and deeper enquiry into spirit-world states (as opposed to heart-felt spirituality itself) will race ahead exponentially from this 21st Century onwards, as it also seems will space-travel and science. Spirit Photography, Electronic Voice Phenomena etc are here just for starters; Parapsychology having already advanced the Psychic Cause in our lifetimes.

Again, actual examples improve on theory, so I'd best

remind of one that took place showing mediumistic ability and psychic energy and which links us with Spirit-World domains and mutual contacts with us:

I was at a Master Charles workshop in Melbourne where he had brought with him from America a highly skilled technician who could set up and read Electro encephalograph apparatus which print out brain wave states. Similar ones read heart rhythms (cardiographs). The Synchronicity organisation created Holo-dynamic Alpha and other state recordings for its followers. It did this with sound waves of different pitches (think of a mother's lullaby singing her baby through progressive layers of sleep, the Alpha one good enough often. Beta being hyperactive, Alpha and Theta achieving more and more restful and creative states, whilst Delta, the lowest Brain Wave State (BWS), would bomb out most folk. Monks can remain awake in that state and be psycho-spiritually active, nevertheless (by degrees and according to the spiritual orders they represented).

I'd never had my brain wave states read, but had naturally been able to get into, it seemed, the highest and the lowest and various permutations of them all. It would make great PhD study for others to make altered states of consciousness their research and theses. I did in part, though it was not easy to find the right universities or freedoms to attend them, with a growing family. My books and own recordings offer whole course material for any would be students of the afterlife, involving Psycho-Spiritual research.

My brain-wave examiner with his and Synchronicity's sophisticated technical apparatus, showed high peaks of all waves as I changed them at will, fascinating him and leaving him non-plussed. I wish he'd given me a print out. But as the

Synchronicity Master Charles implied, he stopped at spirit recognition. Never mind! One day, one day!

Would be students that I mentioned above, would probably find permutated brain wave print-outs in most mediums/psychics they'd need to research. In fact I once helped some students from a nearby university make their basic psychic project film. Some of the information getting through would surely be from the Spirit World. It was all a novel step in the right direction for the students first qualifications, which I hoped they would take further in their careers.

The lasses above showed no fear, even though I said I saw certain spirit folk astrally but also in my home. I'd learned to avoid fright or nervous reaction to this by saying to the students or others, 'It's mainly through clairvoyance, telepathy or astral travel with me, or a mere sense of déjà vu. Also, it doesn't follow that all will see what others see. They may get hunches from time to time but so do most humans. Furthermore, they will pass over one day and long to not be entirely cut off from their families left behind'.

My son David phoned me very recently to say he'd felt a presence only. He seemed disappointed he hadn't seen 'someone', as once before. I'll re-tell his story briefly, though it's in my earlier books, because it's a wonderful innocent, splendid example that surely isn't really 'spooky'.

It may help others acceptance of the perfectly natural fact of 'survival', to realise that we are all spirits and do assuredly live on. I know I will want to watch over all my offspring etc when I return once more to life between lives!

We'd moved from Sydney to a wonderful old home in the Blue Mountains, NSW, built circa 1916 and named *Liege*. A young couple and child selling to us didn't explain why, there was need for modernisation, especially linking to modern sewerage. The old house had a nice big sunroom where I could hold my groups. Next door to it I would set up my study. On its other side was a scullery and the back entrance. The husband, when I mentioned the home had a nice old atmosphere, told me his wife could be seen regularly talking to a nice old lady in old fashioned dress style. He would be in a front room resting after work awaiting his tea and could see them through the half open door. He said it was strange but the wife had adopted the old lady's dress style.

One day after school, quiet young David asked me, 'Did you have a client today Daddy? Because I just saw a lady who seemed to come through the cupboard in the sunroom wall and go through to you in your study, I think'.

I just happened to mention the incident at the local bus stop one day, and a neighbour said 'Yes, your son's right. A bank manager and his wife had lived there, plus her sister'. He was killed in the Granville train smash, his wife now lives elsewhere but the old sister had long passed on.

You can read the longer version and stranger details in my earlier books but the excerpt above is used as a teaching point by me today. Firstly, 'presence'. Just as David feels a presence only, sometimes, I'd felt a presence in Liege, interested in my creating some new decor but respectfully in keeping with the old. Much later I'd look up in a cupboard, way up by the high ceilings and white overalls (men's) and unused rolls of wall-paper were there. The neighbour at the bus top had said he was always decorating. I'd felt that sort of creative 'presence', approving of mine, so I used some of his wallpaper where he might further approve! Back to David and the cupboard:

We examined the red-painted ('disguise') cupboard twixt

the sunroom and the back scullery entrance, where if the shelving were removed, it could easily be seen as a previous door-space between rooms. This at a time when the old lady must have been alive, able to use it and my (eventual) study, plus separate washroom etc and so not disturb her sister and brother in law's rooms.

Readers may conjecture about why in the above non scary, loving family, the older sister remained long, more seen by David and the previous young housewife who took up her style, conversing with her (She would have made a wonderful, most naturally accepting Psychic Medium, as I feel David could). Then there was I, and the once upon a time bank manager, who's pleasant vibes built a 'presence' for me.

I could go on about a group member of mine who used to almost collide with a young looking spirit guy former tenant coming from the bathroom; also a Jewish soul gent who was still earthbound in a house now owned by a woman I met at my GP's; a girl spirit too still visiting her old earth bedroom and turning on the toy gramophone of the then present little boy, who's dog would then take a swift retreat (UK). Earlier a spirit of a little boy who'd tried to rescue a baby bird off his roof but fell and died. Next house purchaser who had no children of her own, consulting me because he was still there and would sit smilingly watching her on her sewing machine (parents sadly having moved on). I couldn't trace them because my own little family had to move on from NZ; most of my passed on loved ones and associates contacting me again in all our/my travels UK to 'down under' and back.

Our fears, orthodoxy led prejudices (inter religious decent cross teachings denied etc) and lack of psycho-spiritual love and understanding, simply deny ourselves and spirit families equally

Please think about it; do!

Hundreds of accounts such as above are written, and far more throughout my book series, if you need more conviction or truthful knowledge. I've been with churches and isms in past lives and been a choirboy but psychically in this one. Nowadays enough evidence has come out for honest acceptance and for religious bias to stop, for our whole human family and heavenly counterparts' truth sake. I now support the CFPSS (Churches Fellowship for Psychical and Spiritual Studies) to whom I currently bequeath my book profits. Why? Because they are an inter-faith, eminently worth supporting, world group; Eastern, Middle Eastern, Western etc.

Its conclusion being that no one organisation has the monopoly on religious life or teaching. Better if like a would be true United Nations; all were represented but in overall respect and protection. No more holy so-called wars.

I may have a more space for the above theme in my Conclusions chapter too. In between I want to entertain and teach readers and would be practitioners of past-life adventures, with more on practice and proof as well as hopeful fascination and evidence.

CHAPTER VIII

Basic training in past-lives induction and recall. Historic details check out later at such as libraries, clothing worn; experiences

I list so many past-life experiences of my own and family, also of friends and clients, throughout my book series, all personally shared with my readers. Regardless of any academic and professional qualification, what better, more relaxing and homely introduction to such an intimate subject, could one have, to teach and guide?

As I refer again to a few fascinating cases in my book series already, they now will be used more briefly, chiefly as instructive, teaching modules.

Psychodrama practice, which largely had its own chapter in this book, taught me a lot, along with other therapies long practiced. It and they figure strongly with my now Karma-Drama title and relevant practice, hereby copyrighted in this book. I will give credit to any related pioneering in my bibliography.

Let us look back to a first past-life experience of my own shortly, so great for a teach-in example. Also, full induction detail as used by me, including my 'secret weapon' – healing type relaxa-energy touch!

As with all my personal altered states of consciousness (ASCs) induction, and any guided imagery for clients, groups etc, it's best in general to lay and relax in a quiet, darkened space, maybe covered lightly according to room temperature (this might help one feel more secure), making certain as much as possible that no phone or anything can disturb. It might even help to put a 'do not disturb' or 'call back later' type note on a door that anyone might knock. Adjust things then as one wants or needs.

One can then listen to a group or personal director, or self-thought or direction, if working alone but experienced in the genre. Or, listen to a trusted prepared, guided recording of instruction, such as those I have created and released online.

Small groups generally

However one is working it may be desirable to use apparatus for recording or even filming sessions. Meditational music if used, should be gentle, relaxing, harmonious, non too intrusively in the background. The directors voice must be clearly heard by all and with gentle but firm control. Also, a second person should be able to take over smoothly if the necessity arises. With larger groups a director could not so easily manage without pairing group members (see below).

Large groups generally

A director might easily manage a large group alone with or without a stand-in, depending on experience, though would need help for such as the megalomaniacal chap's case and that of the 'pregnant male'! However, readers may have picked up for themselves that I made a practice of pairing off group sitters. They would take morning, afternoon or evening sessions, swapping places in turn. Subjects would lay on mats or camp style mattresses whilst the other sat unobtrusively by, writing notes of the reclining one's experience, also gently keeping them in focus, but secondary to the Director's coaching.

A possible second in command could patrol quietly,

teaching the slow couples to focus more. The relaxing therapy person should be given occasional light, intermittent forehead massage by their partner. It's as if to re-charge them (actually it does, helping partners into ever lightened altered states of consciousness (ASCs).

Don't worry, you will learn things in finer detail as I relate actual cases throughout this book and in my previous ones, by degrees, as with use of my relaxation recordings, backing up their particular books with the same title. Also, you will note in this book appendages (see 'Meditational Data' sheet, final pages) how the various brainwave patterns take you down, down, down, deeper and deeper (beta, alpha, theta, delta or mixes though usually only monks can stay awake in or near delta – hence your partner gently calling you back to report things you are seeing, experiencing, feeling.

Relaxation into the necessary altered states of consciousness best begins by a maybe a stretch and a yawn (!), whatever suits one. Then gentle instruction on 'letting go' of body areas and regions singly but fully. Start with gentle commands to relax first whoever's feet fully, be they client, group, or own in private session. Progress then at reasonable pace, relaxation at the ankles, then legs, knees, thighs etc in full dimensions (in other words front back and completely).

One can vary altered states relaxations and doesn't need to be too rigid about preparations but they are so rewarding. I usually gently continue to the back and spinal areas after the lower limbs: -'relax your bottom, lower spine area, upper spinal back area, neck and shoulders. As in hypnosis but with none other than the relaxation guidance, direct that 'you're sinking pleasurably into your mattress' (or whatever's used).

Direction next is to the groin and reproductive area, and

solar plexus Once relaxed, proceed slowly to the lower abdomen etc (oft repeating 'let go, let go -or 'letting go', 'ever relaxing, relaxing'). Again non too obtrusively, directing calmly; peacefully as possible.

Next, reasonably slowly at a time: relax 'tummy in-general/ chest, breast, heart and lungs within, then neck'. (At this stage I usually say 'swallow or scratch if you need to, you'll quickly return to the relaxed position'. Clients/self/whoever, thereby lose tension but ease them back from dropping off to real sleep if necessary! You'll be able to tell. Keep monitoring and gently assuring them plus relaxing, until past lives pop up!).

So! by now clients/self should have stopped from drifting off before being directed to the so expressive face area. Advise then that there are myriads of muscles in the face that show mood or character, to now relax, relax and let go (one can go into detail but ad lib as one thinks fit but keep up the gentle flow; not too much dialogue from you).

Finish off the relaxation with a "Let go at the top of your head and where the head is resting now, and that part of your induction's done".

Continue then by advising how relaxed clients may be by now and relaxing – letting go, with the music. Then direct that we all have body auras – electrical fields that completely surround our bodies, not just our heads and which can be seen by Kirlian photography (one could look up the science and be informed).

The next (but unbroken step as you keep up a nice relaxation) is to instruct clients/groups imaging, 'You're getting pleasantly floaty in your auric fields'. Advise then (whoever's doing the session) to go with the flow and for a brief while before taking off into past lives, practice floating around in your own home or familiar place (but in a dreamy sense of course) say safely onto a garage roof or flat surface or whatever nearby, able to float higher, lower, left, right – any direction you choose. This gets them inspired.

Then will be the time to strike whilst the iron is hot, so to speak. Direct whoever to now practice floating off oh! so safely even further, until they find they can look safely down on Earth. Then to see it spinning back in time gathering speed until days, months, years, decades, even centuries earlier, show up (they are so suggestible at this stage but a reminder that Astronomy can even show us back to the world as it was at any time in the past). Explain then that you're going to count them back down to their personal time and place in their past that they descend to, and learn their karmic lessons from, safely.

Count down occurs then, again safely relaxed, say ten to zero slowly, repeating slowly again if necessary, until similarly to parachutists say, the inductees – single or group – float/floats down slowly and safely, seeing a terrain gradually lighting up. Get them to then keep feeling underfoot what the ground is like. Is it sandy, grassy, rocky, whatever?

Some travellers, into past zones (futures can be tried too) may be unsure at times. Practitioners even conducting their own personal 'trips', may need a few patient count downs. Gradually the past lives encountered will re-live their stories for them (notwithstanding that holistically 'they' are, in part you). It's as if you're in their screen play too, that cannot hurt you, re-absorbing and re-learning from its karmic replay, However, do keep directing the momentum going, by wondering, observing, questioning, probing, searching inquisitively, noting, not giving up, stating the simplest feeling and notion – on what's going on here, so to speak. Eventually 'partners' can begin to take over, raising an arm if Director or stand in director is needed to help.

One should own that all's recorded in our eternal lives and in our very selves presently. It's ours! To claim our right to examine what after all we once were – in that past lives zone, often brings up fantastic, details, answers, healing and growth. Go for it. Don't be timid. The skills of the therapists will draw us out.

Again let me say there is no better specialist learning module than one taught not by good story tellers alone but with those specialised in the practical side of the subjects. Practice makes perfect and by trial and error, if you find other workable variations of my guidelines that suit you, then fine, especially if you are oriented therapeutically.

As in this book's 'Also by Dr Stuart R Rolls, PhD' page, you will find relaxation recordings listed. I might add another sample directly related to this book series (one that I would use in my own Karma Drama/past-life sessions; backed up by the Psychodrama and other broad Therapeutic, plus Psycho-Spiritual knowledge, in my life's mission). However, as I'm only just finishing this book, it might also be that by then I will have time to set up a helpful website. I'd been too busy previously, researching and writing up my book series, over years.

I'll examine again now a few best cases, to help in your own studies of past life adventures of so many present day humans. Do recall that Christ's disciples considered him as a reincarnated John the Baptist. Other faiths too cite similar beliefs about their own founders:

A male nurse, recently divorced, came to me burdened because he'd felt more than an uncommon interest in sex for sale movies. 'Am I turning gay?' he asked, 'and will you help me in a past-life regression, though not with others?' The poor chap seemed hardly able to hide his shame. We proceeded with openness and trust. Induction took about twenty minutes until nonplussed, he felt lost at outback like surroundings but not Australian, possibly some zone in Europe left a bit 'wasted'.

However he 'floated off' to a building which he freely examined, puzzled because down a corridor he saw soldiers' elegant helmets hanging up on equally elegant hooks. He felt he must be a soldier in a Crimean type uniform possibly, but in a hurry, wanted to look inside one of the ornate doors, not the one with 'apparently' other soldiers maybe waiting in it. Then the surprising switch. He felt he was in a woman's body, in a sumptuous gold/white framed bed, ready to offer her services, yes, and wearing the most sensuous under-clothing, perfume and revealing upper gown Wow! Indeed! All worthy of any famous salon fashion of the day, no doubt.

The up-shot was that he came-to amazed, needing to rush home, get over his 'lives' clashing over, and propose to a fellow nurse (female!), who'd long been attracted to him with no success! He a past-life 'Madam no doubt', of late with his sexuality all over the place but now happily in the moment.

Two other Past Life researches I might briefly refer to from my past-life book series, already told but with the author's own authenticity. (Note how one reminds oneself to look diligently for vital detail to return with knowledgeably.)

1. When I counted myself down to terra firma, I was more aware of gentleman in black frock coat and breeches plus buckled shoes. Such shoes I've even bought in this life! I'd watched him walk from an obvious horse and cart, traffic island crossroads. I'd wondered why he'd stopped to check, noise and

clamour whilst walking down a quieter crossroad. He'd been looking down a slope there to a centuries-old looking line of period cottages, where I could just simply sense he usually consulted some kind of clients there (notice how I – the author Stuart, can hardly help slipping from the personal I to He)!

I then, in this later 21st century, walked towards him, found myself stood behind him but then drawn in front of him, with his dark curly hair and dark eyes, looking lost and perturbed, seemingly looking through and past me. I telepathed or somehow received from over-soul that he'd left a loved one behind and was now detecting the said noise and clamour as a Napoleonic era battle force was about to face the British and Allies. Strangely, and being no historian, I was getting little flashes of other battles from around that time too (so may have mixed slight detail).

A lull and I was seeing back a little to the cottage and simply knowing what the footbaths were once all about in there. Mesmer (Anton) whom I was only vaguely now recalling, had been the Father of Mesmerism (virtually raw hypnotism) and I'd once welcomed his expertise there. My clients had experienced his techniques with *healing magnetism, the basis, along with suggestion, of his work.*

I think this was my first past-life regression; self-induced, for I was aux-fait with his/my (?) practice that had been going on at the old cottage. Though only vaguely of pre-Freudian Anton Mesmer.

Each time I pondered a question, it seemed the answers were there with me immediately (trust your 'over-selves' grasp of this intuitive aspect, dear readers).

Back with the swarthy earlier-life me, he was being bayonet prodded with others – no uniforms, into carts, then I was back sharing eternal consciousness with eternal me, to a battle front. The battle name Oudenarde stuck with me. Names of a Marshal Ney and Napoleon himself of course, historically stick in people's memories predominantly, Wellington's name too. Lots of other detail I previously knew nothing of but checked out with library searches later and with a French lady Doctor were verified. Yet, though 'seeing' the battle at Oudenarde, I may have been at Waterloo in whatever incarnation. Therefore we must be extra careful with the evidence when past-lives information appears to overlap.

The above abbreviated account was in my very first of eight of the nine counted with this, my last book of the series, but in fuller details. It offers sound proof, as did another of mine, checked out and proven across the globe by the hallowed Bodleian Library in Oxford, UK.

Just a I foresaw my first wife coming into my present life, I saw my second wife as in her past life with me. We are close again in this life! There's a riddle for readers!

2. One case of Dr Ian Stevenson briefly, took up the story of a young wife in India, married to a Joseph, they serving the Catholic Church. Pride was in their brick bungalow home afforded by the Church, with nearby homes created only from humble wattle and daub.

    A while after the young wife died she reincarnated into another life, in a different mountain fold. As she grew older she kept troubling people insisting she really belonged with a Joseph and she could take them to where he lived. Finally, with Dr Stevenson researching reincarnation worldwide, he decided to take up this Indian case.

The reborn wife (now a teenager) had claimed she could take him to Joseph and the house. Officials of every description went along for the journey which took all day, Finally they had found the right slope, starting to descend the other side when the late young wife, now bounding with overwhelming joy shouted words claiming there was the bungalow. A little later into the descent she had her moment of Eureka, remonstrating that Joseph was there, sitting on his porch!

Joseph wondered what all these people and all this fuss was all about. He hadn't re-married but had no way of recognising the claim that this late teens lass now, of different blood and looks, could have belonged with him once before. In despair she knowingly ran into a room and dug a calico type bag from beneath some tiles there set in sand only. There! She proclaimed, this is where I kept my jewellery with that for the baby we were about to have. Guess what? Joseph and 'she' re-married happily, hopefully this time, for 'ever after'. There were still not too many years between them!

CHAPTER IX

Further instruction in safe learning re in-home practice and Altered States of Consciousness for oneself, and others

This final chapter before Conclusions of maybe final book of what became a series, is meant to help all Psycho-Spiritually. Already you will have learned much from preceding chapters aiding perhaps the more advanced of you professionally/ therapeutically.

If I repeat again and intertwine guidance, safeguards and teachings, they cannot be repeated too often. Reminders are the clinchers, as any educator will tell us, especially when linking more than one discipline. In my case Past Life Research to which I've added and invented the title Karma/Drama, adding to the overall Psycho-Spiritual.

Yet, since I'm still breaking new ground with my avante garde Karma Drama teaching and practice, cautions and new knowledge are here for all, in past lives research and therapy. There really is not much if any formal college, academy, or university training regime at all for you. Just as Grassroots Spiritualism and Psychic Research brought on modern Parapsychology. I hope and trust that they and religions etc espousing reincarnation will adopt my titles – *Karma Drama: Reincarnation and re-setting your Karma* – though it could be a sub title of related disciplines in the Psycho-Spiritual domain.

However, from gentle beginnings, do take in my advice and

tips below, from my own, wife Sheila's plus clients own past lives. Hopefully for readers, the wonderful accounts from other's experiences, not just mine/ours, will help and impress. I cannot repeat reminders often enough, some of the guidelines and cautions below.

Therapists/Practitioners/others, if new to Karma Drama etc, should bring clients/sitters back to present time carefully, gently, when they are ready. This especially where there has been seeming (but time past) untoward behaviour; also because of the fact that they are assimilating and learning from that past, but now assuredly from a safe place.

I would arrange, as already explained, for group members, doing a session each in turn, to not interfere with the busy Therapists/Practitioners overall instructions, but as said – as group-leaders/helpers. To give close comfort and encouragement to the 'tripper' (as explained elsewhere), to say what they were experiencing: Continuing then with such as 'leave the bad things in the past now but learn by them. Cherish and learn by the good things too'.

If 'helpers' get no co-operation raise their hands to attract Group leaders. If 'trippers' seem stuck encourage them to keep on researching, look at every detail, question if night or day, place, situation, weather, relationships, happenings, everything, and know they can understand people in the past and see what they were doing, as if in the present moment. Keep moving (a bit like as in Psychodrama's 'surplus-reality').

You see mainly the memories when past life 'tripping'. It's largely about you and what happened to you as your old self, from and with others, in habitats and places as they were. By analogy it's like watching movies you get engrossed in and reflectively see what was said and done. By analogy, home and other movies can nevertheless show and be way back from the past too.

No! you don't really converse or re-enact with that past, but again by analogy, your past-life memory can 'see' and relate far back in the Universe's 'personal' history. After all, your past lives would have been spent in and at correspondingly different 'times' in the Universe. It's postulated there are others! Which one's might we have been in?! Astronomers can tap into the Universe's total past life too. You wouldn't want to go back to the Big Bang though, would you?! Human's weren't around then!

So the corollary of all the above is, if we humans can 'see' the Big Bang in its cosmic time, or one day other Big Bangs elsewhere possibly. Where then and what are we? One conclusion we may draw is that we are in the Eternal 'now' of everlasting constant flux! Part of everything, including material/spiritual/change and interchange, to higher forms or spiritual 'beingness', in Eternity. Putting it simply we are all part of the whole

Back to associates etc from past lives on our planet (and maybe on others) they may not converse directly with us -our being like cinema-goers looking in, but we can engage with them in soul essence and re-enact with them in a Psychodrama surplus-reality type of way. Prayer of course can always be used, for anything and everything in infinity and Eternity, we being part of the whole, in which all is known in its 'flux'.

(See Swedenborg's *Heaven and Hell* (in bibliography), somewhat supplementary to my bridging things philosophically.)

Back to chapter heading: For practitioners of course, I've already cautioned about short circuiting clients or group members minds carelessly whilst they're in suggestible or altered states of mind or consciousness. This applies in Hypnosis (or Mesmerism as I've shown in my other lives), Psychodrama, past-life sessions etc.

E.g., 'you'll fall over backwards with laughing'; or say 'you'll cry till the cows come home'; or more seriously 'you'll be able to jump chasms'. Only the possible, non dangerous, helpful, not able to be misconstrued, is practitioner worthy.

Reaction to past lives should be about recognising how the past affected you, seeing the good but now finding growth from the not so good. Later sessions may take one back to use Psychodramas' Surplus Reality techniques etc, if any negative stuff still bothers. Yet many not so good affectations melt into general feeling of 'hang-ups' 'overseen' – but quite interesting to say the least. I've quoted a few e.g., avoidance tactics at not being a vagrant or loner anymore, put in stocks, an entertainer at some noble court, having to keep one's head by not being caught up in intrigue; a wariness about over softness and being used, etc.

We never feel the pain of our past-life passings etc, though we may have 're-visited' and 're-witnessed them'. Now past-lives lovers might strike up different chords! Some folk would say, shame it's all in the 'mind'!

Generally, I recall how at residential school, lads were always up to tricks. One way in particular was that certain of the pupils would separately home in on another, saying things like 'you look sick today', or 'how pale you are', 'you must be in pain by the way you look', 'watch you don't vomit', is anything the matter with you?', 'you look very shaky', etc. By the time the poor subject got to sick bay he'd be so near fainting or falling over, he'd be put to bed.

Then there are the super-market subliminals, TV subtle images – suggestibility everywhere abounding, not forgetting those stage hypnotists, though positive thinking messages can come in many ways too.

Charismatic leaders can inspire nations. In sports etc, coaches guide one. Much 'guided imagery' can be used; by therapists including those in training too It mightn't be too helpful to be told 'you'll run till you drop', 'don't stop for anything', or, say if you're dieting – 'go till your pants fall down' (joking)!

Émile Coué (Coueism) would teach repeating in gradual re-enforcing stages, such as – 'Hour by hour, day by day, I get better in every way' – where you can also pick a subject, sport, behavioural matter, whatever (for upgrade suggestions to yourself). Silently or verbally.

Again, you know what I mean by keep to positive thinking; refuse being misled; avoid ambiguity.

Now, in our case, vet what gets planted into our thoughts. A good practitioner should avoid carelessly/loosely addressing our fertile minds whilst we're off guard, or being too trustingly over relaxed.

Rumour too, can so easily affect us and nowadays we have to be so careful with social media as well as mainline media. Salesmanship too can be a very vexed subject

There! I trust I've light heartedly helped persons who take up any sort of personal analysis, relaxation technique – indeed mind control. I do advise again, working with conscientious, able, caring practitioners first.

Again 'The readiness is all', as I often quote from Hamlet. Beginners at whatever stage in Psycho-Spiritual healing knowledge, where most can be thought of as beneficial, need ideally to attend other groups, sittings, or teach-in workshops. Gradually you'll attain comfort, help and growth, at whatever pace.

As already advised, Psychodrama and other mixes of therapies, psychological wisdom, also practice, will advance you personally in all round health and life. You may wish to become a practitioner having first 'practiced' with therapists or in therapy groups etc, with safe quality or aims

Ethical consideration

I do advise you to take advantage of the Psychodrama etc in this book chapter VI. It will properly ground, help, train and prepare you. Further teachings, you now may obtain in your preferred format (print, ebook and audio) via many online retailers. Therefore I advise you not to practice alone too hurriedly or unprepared (find a partner if possible). You've a wonderful primer in Chapter VI here, not to skip but read and practice over and over for support. Guidance is also throughout this series with all I've written or recorded Psycho-Spiritually. Don't give up though and do get a look in first on appropriate group activities if ready

Even so, therapists do work on themselves alone sometimes. I did, but the therapy word covers a lot of ground. 'Soul-therapy' takes in past lives and old karma, within my new Karma Drama teaching. It leads to higher-order, spiritual-heavenly, states of life; soul-karmically achieved. Far 'beyond' so called astral and other planes. No rush, for it's Eternity we're talking about here!

We will no doubt look higher still in my Conclusions, to possible, everlasting destiny or fate for all!

CHAPTER X

Conclusions

Ah! My conclusion! At this stage I usually type 'epilogue', as a short appendage commentary writing piece etc, though usually there's so much to say and finish with at the end of a book in a series, that 'conclusion' says it better, this time. There is more a sense about a finish with this book anyway, because it does finalise the 'Psycho-spiritual', 'unintended whole series', explained earlier. It covers such an extant continuum.

Getaway to Down Under was a separate steamy, romantic, novel, though it was based on truth, travel and psychic happenings, making up now my authorship of nine books.

I've spent so much time catching up on my own childhood predicted psychic mission, writing and further researching my books. Now I will have more time to spend publicising them more, their truths being so worthy but thanks to my co-operative spirit guides. They've collectively shown and taught me so much, giving me experiences of all the 'spiritual gifts' and predicting I would write them up for humanity.

Before I wrote these books, I used to send articles to psychic newspapers and magazines, but haven't had time to spare for these or to develop social media skills, or a website. Therefore I get very little recompense back from publishing them online. Do consider sending them your valued 'likes'. They give you samples to read and recommend, if you wish. It's for my cause, not just me. Who would not want to have their spirit mission valued good, neutrally and humouredly, rather than have it devalued by so many competing, intimidating, world dogmas.

My readers know how entertaining and evidential the Psychic and Paranormal can be, as wonderful stories of loved ones gone on before dispelling our silly fears. It's so delightful that proof of survival comes through to us this way. Mine's a mission but I'm so glad of it as a privilege A lifetime of 'magical' psychic happenings have been mine for the asking. I'm so lucky and glad to have had my family and a loving spiritual initiation at my dear Mom's psychic knee and her mother's psychic experience inheritance too, bequeathed now for all for my readers).

In my own psychic/spiritual blessings I've kept down to Earth though was taken by guides to visit another planet (reported in this book). We can't do these things alone, I'm sure, nor would I be conceited enough to think so (see Indian Swamis book on other planets in bibliography).

Maybe I've deserved a holiday with my family in England again, at long last. I have a family here in Australia also. My books tell how wonderful and varied the psychic experiences I've had over a lifetime, 'back home', 'down under' here in Australia and also in New Zealand.

Currently, I'm interested in bequeathing all my writings and all profits to humankind through an Inter-Faith Movement. Just think, with members from all religions invited etc invited to their ranks; how wonderfully international is that!? It could be the Churches Fellowship for Psychical and Spiritual Studies (CFPSS) or some other I might find.

I despair at the world sometimes but am proud of the young to whom we all hand over in turn.

Incidentally, I say again, more than once now, the CFPSS inter-faith organisation are open to anyone, who regardless of members' religions are open to each other's in multi-faith respect. That's a great bonus, these somewhat radicalised days, isn't it folks? Do support them

Anyway, I hope my books and recordings help and please many. They tell how we can heal and bless all, without over stuffy, self centred organisations. I belong to none but all faiths where they/we can meet. 'Love is all you need'.

In researching Eastern beliefs, faiths, wisdoms and practices (especially for *East–West Paranormality*) it was obvious that worldwide, humankind mainly thinks, philosophises and believes much the same, anyway. Increasingly too, it begins to think there is something in belief in the afterlife and possible coming back reincarnation). Respecting worldwide different emphases is the key. Across the globe we all have family members or know someone who is psychic, delineating things perhaps according to their own culture. Now why do we often go on and spoil it all?

True! Genes, national prejudice, custom, state of body and mind, too – whatever, will currently affect our judgement. However, Karma Drama as originally named and presented by me now (you might agree) offers wonderful, insightful, self-evidence for ourselves. With it we'll personally know the Paranormal, Parapsychological, Space Age and Quantum thinking overall, Psycho-Spiritually for ourselves.

Its late now and I need a cuppa etc, so let's pick up in the morning – agreed? This Conclusion is going to be longer!

Morning duly arrived! I need to get more philosophical in closing, now that I've related so much of my psychic life and its implications. I leave religion aside now, apart from the inter-faith or neutral, worldwide. May I reinforce again, no one has control rights or monopoly of our souls, past-life belief or states, or our reincarnational lives to come (same thing really!). It's up to us how we travel in our soul growth and how we earn it, in higher States as yet hardly seen or dreamt of.

Nevertheless, I was so happy as a little choir boy singing his heart out; linking years later when I was home once, with grandson Christopher and his choirs entrance at, I think, Kings College, Cambridge, England.

Well! We go through enlightening stages. I've hopefully stretched my readership with mine and so many other persons past lives recall, also contact with loved ones in spirit now. I've had my driving sense of lifetime mission. I struggled with degrees and diploma's etc to back things up and give my basically reserved self, more credence.

I notice brilliant Professor Brian Cox, thinking materially much like brilliant Professor Stephen Hawkins (bless them), has visited Australia. He tells us that from the Southern Hemisphere, we have the clearest world views of space, the Milky Way and billions and billions of stars – billions, deemed impossible years ago! That's crept up on us over the years of advancing astronomy; space age and quantum physics plus other things that weren't 'there' when I was a lad (but like most things, just waiting to be seen, acknowledged and believed in)!

Yet once born into this life again, albeit in my present loving family, I knew in my freshly experiencing boyhood soul, that space and variances within it, and so called heavenly bodies forming and re-forming, so to speak, went on forever. One just couldn't drop off into a perpetual void. We just can't have an abstract nothing -no separate thing, not a breath or a 'being'!

Our Astronomers above, in their present lives (because

they'll come back too – reincarnate!), may still intellectually be hooked into examining the physical heavens, more than the spiritual counterpart of everything. Yet they're doing a great job and playing their part in the overall of what is or might be.

For now, more and more astronomers say, 'we just don't know', re the more eternal and forever reach of space. That's so gratifying after all the past limited, denial views of the physical eternity, not to mention a spiritual one. Sure planets, orbs, worlds etc, collide, explode and are no more as such.

Now let me ask some rhetorical questions: Where do those physical/material 'have beens', including space debris, previous gas clouds etc, all constituent parts, go? Surely into cyclical re-building of something else – surely in the context of – wait for it -physical reincarnation! Even black holes lead to somewhere! So! Even materiality is never lost, nor can our spiritual beingness ever be lost, surely?

But then, though we begin to grasp the eternality of all things, we might ask what of those rocks, gases, dusts, other properties, sun-sized stars, planets, even some with human, plant and animal type life aboard – if sucked into those black holes? Surely they will survive anew, in some other form, somewhere in Eternities Eternal properties and rounds?

Now back to Spirit life, astral-planes, belts, spheres, Heavens and any other life places or states denied too, except by we so called simple and faithless (try 'inter-faith the noo', as the Scots say).

Whatever state we think the after-life state is, then, if we come back from it, (reincarnate), it must have been something spiritual!

We used to think the world was flat once!

With my books and recordings I think I've proven the ever cycling spirit – no not just that of the Tour De France!

It's logical now to think beyond flat earth thinking and also now of planets – whole galaxies, material life, everlastingly denied having an evolution, as in the broader sense we have.

I ventured into quantum physics and science a little in my book series so far. I've more than ventured into our spiritual life, here and hereafter. I've philosophied too about Godly/Spiritual views, East–West etc, no Earthlings having the monopoly of either. The magnitude of all those surely endless stars and planets etc, re-cycling, dwarf everything eternally. This along with our ever recycling/ reincarnating selves, not forgetting some of our own higher beings per se, now advanced to higher states so far ahead of us, where we'd possibly feel out of place.

Books like 'Back to Godhead' in my Eastern readings, point out that we mightn't always be physical, human type planetary beings but be progressively more 'angelic' and of higher spirit. Everything evolves, one sees.

Let us get on with living one life at a time, ever amazed at our every step. It's the conjecture that's forever opening up Eternity for us, and in it we should rejoice, ever research, progress, love, share and be happy. Not bad maxims for now, whatever 'now' indicates eternally.

Finally let me say because we're in that 'now', as in my earlier books of the series, let's make the best of it Psycho-Spiritually. It helps to think of that 'now' concept as eternal change – nothing lost (both in the physical and the spiritual). Also, the more we open up, we have measurement and predictiveness about forever change happening upon us and around us. It's as though we're currently and largely stuck in one dimension – time, though it's relative (see Einstein).

In terms of the human psyche however, proven prophecy seems to indicate that the future is already here in some way, and in the philosophical 'now' of the grand scheme of things! Some thinkers agree it's already happened, the corollary being that we're now in a re-run of some sort! I've made the proposition myself that true prophecy of itself would seem to indicate that the future has already happened! Now there's another mystery for my valued readers to be entertained by if not perplexed!

Be guided and maybe read up more on that 'now', as I myself 'come down to Earth'. One last thing: regarding astral planes, as eternal, as in endless space maybe; some are relative to our present 'now' and current evolution, hopefully 'heavenly', in a manner of speaking. They seem to meld with Earth, as in some of my experiences, it being as though some Earthlings I'd known, hadn't quite crossed over (see rest of this series). Perhaps the 'now' is just like an ever unrolling scroll, the past being wound up say by some mystical left hand (having already served its purpose) and the future being unwound more clearly (for prophecy) by the right hand! We can only then reflect on the past but do something reflectively about the future!

Grassroots psychics have long held 'recue groups' to help 'lost spirits' move on. I've done a bit of this work individually and it's so rewarding to get them to concentrate on joining their friends and family gone on before Possibly other astral -plane areas are as blank as unevolved planets.

After this 'series' and researches I've undergone, over so many years (this and other lives personally researched psycho-spiritually), I'll think about that holiday! Peace, Progress and Blessings to All!

Finally, after this Conclusion Chapter, I will add as bonus some informative interesting repeat article etc, as in the rest of the series, but also some new ones, plus a final poem as in other books of the series, as yet unwritten. 'Over' dear readers, with my, the author's, Blessings.

CHAPTER XI

Review

Currently I've been gathering more helpful and stimulating psychic articles for readers to educate us more, perhaps on wider world issues. Some of mine as extra bonuses from earlier books in my psycho-spiritual series, have turned out to be quite prophetic, in particular about China, Russia, USA and ourselves and of course the rest of the world, in keeping the peace. Two or three new articles are with approval from the weekly website of Victor and Wendy Zammit here in Australia, though of course reaching out worldwide over the internet. Readers can also find out their Facebook, various other outlets and personal website details, back of this book. Folk will do themselves a favour reading of their so busy and informative, blessed, psychic works, going for many years now, graciously and freely non-stop. There's a lot of bonus wealth there.

One of the articles alluded to above is not about China's miraculous growth but the growth of many of its children by the multi thousands, in its State sponsored psychic training and development:

THE US GOVERNMENT ACKNOWLEDGES PSYCHIC POWER IS REAL is a second article as headed by Victor Zammit which I've included in my extras at the back of my book. He pointed out the multi US intelligence gathering by psychic means ('remote viewing' etc. I've mentioned in my book series too). Victors article goes on to mention The US Joint

Chiefs of Staff, the Secret Service and vital other agencies privy to said 'remote viewing' etc. Wow! I never thought as a young Spiritualist and later Parapsychologist, the world would come to this (this is why I like to add. the word Spiritual when I'm writing about myself or work as Psycho-Spiritual).

Further to the above, Victor was a solicitor at High Courts of State and Federal level and has written his own book as you may note in my Bibliography. However, in his articles his brilliant mind foresees the risks of misuse of paranormal powers by whomsoever States. I have to add this would not be Spiritual for humankind. But! 'To be forewarned is to be forearmed.'

I now want to re-enforce what I've written before about Prophecy and can it be seen as of the certain future already and inevitable, or as in the forewarning only category, above paragraph. Or (because I wanted to make this a light-hearted and breezy chapter), is prophecy something we can merely predicate as connote, suggest, logical or implication? Well! There was a time when things were hot, long ago, between now happier China and the rest of the fear ridden world. It may have been mentioned in my first book that I had a very clear vision of four atom bombs being dropped at strategic points, along her (China's) coastline, but humankind's common-sense prevailed and halted that awful possibility (thank all that's sacred). So! From this we can deduce that some prophecies can be scary but seen as warnings.

Prophecy does prove to be absolutely or even partially accurate often. So many true accounts are in my books. People are so gullible sometimes that it behoves us all to explain our psychic renderings helpfully, without too much conjecture. Yet I'm sure that in our lives there are powers that can overcome evil or wrongdoing (Saints or Godly figures if one likes). I tend to think of it all as of 'Higher Spirit'. Again see Bibliography and elsewhere in my book series. My guides (gurus if you like, customarily), are always feeding me more knowledge.

Light-heartedly now about prophecy and mediumship, I've had fun with foreseeing my various grandchildren's boy or girl status, successfully. Yet I made a mistake with one here in Australia. Son David and his dear wife Sheree (though she 'goes me' if I spell her name wrongly; hope it's right this time or I'm for it!) had the blessing of a sweet little baby girl over a year ago. As I live miles away up in the Blue Mountains, NSW, her Mommy kindly brought her up to see me early on in her dear little life.

David's been so busy, learning his company management (JP too), that he helps me more in health emergencies I've been having. However, he usually visits with his more mature also lovely daughter and his cute little five-year-old blondie lass. Anyway, I'd misread the signs, thinking the new baby would be a boy (this ties in with above paragraphs about prophecy). My prophetic vision for David and Sheree was of a darker short-haired, possibly new baby boy. Oops! Maybe this was what I'd hoped for her parents. Also I see her on Facebook months later with short hair and I answered others there who'd thought she was a boy with a proud 'she's gorgeous'! It's hard not to misinterpret sometimes but maybe she will be a lovely little tomboy one day. I've mentioned all my family members in my book series, also some of their psychic happenings, but as appropriate to the time of writing. We don't want to grandstand but we are a psychic family overall that can illustrate the whole psycho-spiritual case for our fellow humans.

I'm showing my age now but the photo of me on the back cover was taken only weeks ago. Here and there in my books, photos as early as the times written in, will most often be shown. Also I'm sure I will have written on most if not all of my extended family, whom I would have shared my psychic gifts and knowledge with. Dr Bill Spence, one of my own tutors in my various psycho-spiritual studies and research (Psycho-drama), years ago, thought me a great tutor, but needful of getting over my own disturbed childhood. Well! I do date back to the Second World War period and have variously been advised, now that I'm an author, to attempt an autobiography. OK!

Researching, writing and planning for the tenth book finally, which inclusive of the suggested subject above, will I suppose, not be without some psychic content, for I'll bring it all up to date through the years. Readers, clients, etc. have so advised I should do this, though I'm a little reserved still in my personality. Yet this has helped me in understanding my fellow humans and wanting to help them and the world in whatever way I can. One can look back in the book series and read how my kind (also psychic) wartime disabled school teacher, prophesied for me at my then age of only ten, that it was my life's personally chosen mission to come back from the afterlife. This as an eventual psychic tutor, writer and healer. I don't think my kind teacher mentioned the mental health healing aspect of it all then, which no doubt will come up in the proposed autobiography too. Nor could he have known much then about forthcoming Parapsychology, new research Altered States of Consciousness and Mediumship, and how healing-type energies (psychic and spiritual) could and would reinvigorate psychic practitioners.

I will write too about surviving a war, boyhood evacuation, taking the Mickey out of Mr Hitler, having a boys' band with my brothers – two back from British Army and Navy service, one was involved in delivering tanks and men on 'D Day' with the British navy. Later he was initially sailing for Australia, ending up being diverted to rescue emaciated, Colonial Dutch prisoners and others from the departing Japanese soldiers, in now called Indonesia. The other older brother (British army driver) ended up in Greece, dodging multi bomb craters on the mountain roads up from Athens and the port of Salonika, delivering mail etc. World peacetime again with no food rationing and finally getting 'down under' years and years later, should appear in the proposed autobiography. All that just for starters, so perhaps I'll go ahead and write this, it having such wide historic as well as family importance; some fun too.

I feel I should impart a little now light-heartedly on understanding religion more. Not by criticism in any way for I simply have proof from the Bodleian Library in Oxford UK (Church of England records) that I was once one of their Ministers – see other books in the series. A medium in Auckland NZ rendered this knowledge, it taking me years to check it out with that fine Institute.

Let us neutrally ponder now some meaning to life and guidance from it. There are so many religions, cults, ways of life and philosophies to choose from. Much depends on which country we were born in. Is it accidental or soul need, karma driven or what? (In the latter there are explanations and analogies of schooling – the soul forever learning by earthly experience and beyond.) Long live the differences I say, having made a practice of looking into past lives and reincarnation. It all figured logically as well as spiritually. Some of the past lives re-visited psycho-spiritually and with modern parapsychology ramifications, offer wonderful proofs and truths. From grassroots Spiritualism onwards and presently, we gain so much proven knowledge of the Afterlife and our loved one there in between lives. Obviously we don't learn all we can from one life.

Church of England choirboy days were a joy for me but I always sensed there was so much more beyond (not so much the altar wine I naughtily stayed behind to swig from a cupboard bottle!). Oh dear! Albeit I loved the services, the dogma barely affected what I soul or spirit knew. I loved the singing also and felt 'oh! well, this is the English way! Romans have theirs; the Asians, Indians and Martians too!' Naughty me! Joking apart, I took to all the C of E customs like a mature Vicar (past-life recall no doubt) and was variously given the job of carrying the cross or lighting and extinguishing the alter candles.

Readers, perhaps you'll agree, we need to think for ourselves but we can surely appreciate there is so much more non parochially for us to understand. In my last book, *East–West Paranormality*, I examined Middle-Eastern religions too, amongst the world's major six or seven. Though naturally having their different supreme beings, deities and ways of worship, I found they all came up with much the same views on afterlife/past lives. As modern science and logic re-evaluates things more in this century understanding faiths differently, it's hoped that as we've matured to Leagues of Nations, United Nations and other International groupings, we may advance to Spiritually United Nationship. Inter-faith movements are growing.

My one time wartime army brother and wife, once settled in NZ awhile. They thought some holy spirit was sending them messages one night via knocking on their only newly rented house walls. After a night of lost sleep they discovered the noise was due to a possum in their wall cavities! How easily we humans get carried away. Though tired, it must have raised a few laughs.

Finally let us speculate about Gods or Ultimate Cause, after the above fun, which, as being mere human in a wondrous nature and starlit space all around, we certainly didn't create. We go on pondering the question 'who or what did'? Some organisations name that 'what' as 'Eternal flux' (Professor Haldane), others such as the Synchronicity Foundation, USA, nominate all as 'Source', 'First Cause' with no implied Creator or Inspirer, is another descriptive way of looking at our 'being'. Everything is just here, there, everywhere, tautologically. Fresh minded babies upwards to more reasoned ages, don't even think about it all. One day they might or will, especially if and as they recall past lives (starting points to begin all over).

I keep refining my own book views to all above. Perhaps we will all find our way back to Source, enriched by various planetary existence; needs of material karma closed and superseded. What's in a name!? If not many Gods – perhaps a godly super spirit chain of command! We surely aren't ready enough (like those children above), though past lives experience and super readiness might even let them surpass most of us. It's not a race. There's no hurry, no real concern. Let's all relax, one step at a time. Enjoy the moment and the journey!

We humans are still very immaturely reactive. Why fight about differences when all about us can be resolved, but this is what we need to learn. Tit for tat earthliness can surely be replaced by our better qualities. All those songs about peace and all we need is love swell up in our hearts from time to time but 'the thought is father to the deed' and we will get there! It is a potentially more wonderful world. Better still by our accepting that our loved ones live on and we will renew our acquaintance and rejoice with them, the better we all utilise our Karma/ Drama.

In final Review now I'm co-operating with Spirit (I was about to state 'Higher Spirit' but I feel our spirit guides and helpers are the ones that interpret knowledge for us from that level of continuum). I arose and started typing earlier than usual this morning, tired after being so influenced to make finalising notes all night. I'd get my torch and scribble information quickly. It was the same at early bedtime, struggling three or more times to delay my sleep for the sake of pencilling the gist of what is in this and any following paragraphs of this chapter. I mislay or can't read my own sleepy jottings sometimes, but by and large they're mostly about those ASCs (altered states of consciousness).

I'm influenced to now show the difference of approach between mine and my spiritual guides' afterlife, rebirth, psychic and karmic teaching etc, and such as at organisations like Synchronicity, Lucid Dreaming and Monroe Institutes, USA. The institutes and similar foundation more or less stop when it comes to the greater concerns of psychic organisations starting with basic spiritualism leading to parapsychological research. Lucid dreaming releases subjects into the art of fantastic 'trips' similar to how we in Spiritualism astral travel. So do the other altered states of consciousness organisations, broadly. They've utilised these states and come up with their own specialisations.

Master Charles, founder of Synchronicity, as mentioned in my books earlier, came close to psychic phenomena when his brainwave expert technician did recordings of my brainwave patterns at a Melbourne workshop they'd set up here in Australia. I, as many others can, could create healing power by the laying on of hands. Further, my speciality was developing hypnotic inducing energies (for psychotherapy or past life research) also through my hands. Both would have shown bursts and spikes of altered brainwave states and I kept giving bursts of energy this way, which baffled the expert. I do wish Synchronicity had given me a print-out and studied psychic phenomena more. Master Charles said it all with a grin when I later tried to talk psycho-spiritually with him. 'Stuart, I know nothing about spirits.'

Nevertheless, those organisations above offer so much about the diversity of experience and knowledge our minds and spirits can lead us to. Like the Buddhists and other religious groupings they are all about the altered states that give us so much respite from the everyday. Joy, peace and understanding follow. 'Live and let live' the more in the world and beyond, some to their eventual Nirvana, of whatever description. What matter the world, even Universe experience. 'Be one with the experience.' 'Be one with the Infinite.' By it our souls link with all other souls (soul mates, twin souls, group souls included?). All one with the Godly or Eternal, whether we believe in a supreme being or that eternal ever creative flux, no beginning or end, or not. Such hallowed belief may be thought of in different ways throughout the Universe and/or multi Universes. Our soul learning and karma is surely not over yet. Surely anything Super human or Divine would patiently allow us the clarion call 'The Universe is unfolding as it should'.

At the end of this review now readers, let me request, do make time for meditation, in group as well as on one's own. In group experience one can hardly feel alone. The shared joy brings about altered states of such bliss and soul togetherness. Instead of making war or un-spiritual difficulties for anyone we deem less than ourselves, we let the diplomacy of fellowship begin. Feelings can open out to join with all sorts of other groups and amalgamations, eventually with all humanity, groups within groups, unto Eternity itself. 'All One' then, there can be no such thing as truly 'Other', spiritually speaking. I myself must get back to meditation ('soul hearkening') I call it, now that my exhausting writing mission over years is almost concluded. Phew!

A couple of TV programmes haven't quite let me go, my having been reticent and struggling only to freethinkingly philosophise, not getting involved in religious preaching or argument. In the first – I have to say beautiful programme – a look was taken at the ancient world and types and views of Gods and on the fates delivered by them, with fore-warnings seen in certain omens (weather patterns, failed crops etc). Propitiations and sacrifices were made necessary to please these Gods or powers, thus to invoke their pleasure and better treatment. Many could be seen as Guardians or predictors of all the fates, weather, battles, etc.

In ancient Egypt where there had been many Gods created, also according to human thinking and superstition, in particular, a Sun God was totemised. However, Tutankhamen's father, needing to hang on to the power of absoluteness, played the Gods down and started his own God-like divine rule. The boy son, so young at his father's death, was easy meat for Egyptians of worldly political power, ready to manipulate back other Gods, as of old. It was easy for them to take over wasn't it and all very mortal?!

Finally here, I watched a TV talent show last evening. A young immigrant lass – a lovely singer from Africa, left viewers with this sweet but deep saying, which they call Abuntu in her country of origin; namely the saying was:

'I am, because you are.'

My friend Gerry Johnston must be given credit here for urging me to write this extra chapter (he knows my work). Also whilst I've been flat out completing a massive multi book series mission, living alone, facing operations etc and doing everything for myself (daughter Jennie arriving from England too for a while to look after her 'Daddy'). Gerry would support me with my computer and printer problems (see his letter of support for me in my last book *East–West Paranormality*.

Now on to Addendum …

ADDENDUM

Being the last book of a series, more total guidance will be found in the nine overall (one, though rather hot in novel form was somewhat psychic and yet truth based).

This book has been about our life and our life hereafter. It has shown soothingly how to relax in these pursuits. I've covered the psychic and spiritual, taking everyone along with me.

My main insights to impart were about the entering of altered states of consciousness (ASCs), for anyone, so revealingly/peacefully. The case histories/accounts being seemingly beyond us. This is where practitioners of many disciplines come in. I've practiced in many areas too, so have guided them and come up with multi cover of my own, and named it 'Karma Drama'.

Practitioners/therapists, you've been introduced now to multi discipline approach and noted how I've used this. You will find your own balance from your own therapies. E.g., suggesting only the methods of relaxation to clients, obviously not the content of their 'trips'. Your skill will be in getting them to seek and see things for themselves.

There's much more in the use of psychodrama than this book portrays. If you're not too familiar with the subject, it will really enhance your work. You'll have noticed that in most 'trips', interrogating protagonists isn't necessary. Wait but question to ourselves. We're only onlookers to our historic selves. Yet if the desire to hit back is overwhelming – though it's 'unreal', it may help within ourselves and 'the moment' to use a 'surplus reality' criticism, if only mentally. So! In practice, adaption is your key, to which I add my blessings.

ARTICLES

The following articles universally relevant to this day, along with the author's timeless poems, are helpful to practitioners, clients, readers and the healing-arts for humankind. Stuart specifically requested that publishers repeat and pass on as bonus for All.

COPY OF ARTICLE TO BLUE MOUNTAINS ECHO

RELIGION AND PSYCHOLOGY

by DR STUART ROLLS PhD

Religion and psychology grew out of the nebulous regions of philosophy enquiring into the nature of being. Such search led variously around the world and throughout history to postulations about deities.

Churches are emptying at an alarming rate. Social mobility eases expectations laid upon us in closer knit communities. During darker ages religion was enforced by the cruel rack, other diabolical tortures and unholy 'holy wars'. Even nowadays, religious groups murder each other all around the world.

Despite war and disunity with religion, awe, pride and nostalgia attend memories of my choirboy days in England. Yet!

Somehow it wasn't quite enough and seemed elitist when migrants from Asia started to arrive in my city with their different gods but still the one Divine Source, surely? Also, I was later working in other, then unliberated institutions (psychiatric) still in their dark ages, keeping the human spirit captive.

Earlier in USA but later in Australia, social conditions brought together disparate religious, ethnic and racial groups, in one community. Human kind with all its questings into what is reality, has never had such a fraternal, multi-cultural chance to look at God and the Cosmos anew.

Infinite space must surely present other intelligences with their regions ideas of deities and wayshowers, light years from our splintered 'holier-than-thou' groupings. However, perhaps in the wake of America's multi-cultural experience, comes from California, Transpersonal Psychology, working in the spirit and not just with mind and body.

Parapsychology has more the scientific proving of the 'spiritual gifts' (as in Corinthians 1.12, St Paul) than the more subjective humanistic, experiential Transpersonal Psychology but both show these gifts are not for the monopoly of the churches or indeed anyone's.

Healing, prophecy and psychic powers are independent 'gifts' to develop, though ideally should be guided spiritually, in the true sense of the word.

Evolution and change are in the nature of things. In the face of empty church pews the spiritual findings of the New Age Psychologies could interface excitingly with Australian multi-cultural religious revival. What a blessed psycho-spiritual renaissance for all!

Author's Footnote:

The Blue Mountains communities have developed ribbon-like along the Great Western Highway and Railroad. Churches have fought for prominence vehemently and often divisively. The above article was contributed to the Blue Mountains Echo's religious debate and was well received.

The climate is surely right in this Aquarian age for the Psycho-Spiritual revival alluded to.

BROCHURE

STUART ROLLS PhD.
Blue Mountains and Sydney

ESP – RE-BIRTHING – TRIPS – PAST LIVES – KARMA-DRAMA – ALTERED STATES – EVERYDAY COUNSELLING & PSYCHOTHERAPY

Rationale: Psychoanalytical therapies gave way to Humanistic Psychology and the Psychedelic Revolution's quest for self-experienced knowledge of our minds, psyches, souls. Such experiential insight and growth – but non narcotically, is now the way of safe Transpersonal Psychology, integrating holistically, emotional, physical, intellectual and spiritual wellbeing. Such integration is denied and 'mind-blowing' risked without a trained therapist. Altered states of consciousness (ASCs) 'trips', ESP and healing – especially psycho-spiritual, are beautifully attained relaxing to thera-pist/guide's instruction, imagery, inspiring music, coordinated with breath, yoga, 'Christos', 'Gemini' or other techniques.

Maslow, Grof, Orr and other transpersonal psychologists recognise that phobias, fears, problems, neuroses – even psy-choses can disappear after spiritual and mystical states, 'highs', 'peaks', etc., once upon a time superstitiously punished or pathologised.

In Transpersonal Psychology amazing clarity illuminates

hang-ups or therapeutic understandings of ourselves in what we call 'the present', in the Cosmos, or, takes us time-travelling – enlightening even 'beyond ego' (Professor Vaughan). All depends on where our priorities, needs and evolutionary states are and as glimpsed perhaps in the following revealing quotations: 'The readiness is all', Hamlet; 'In my beginning is my end', Elliot; 'Infinity is the palm of your hand', Blake; or, Biblically, Corinthians 1.12, 'to some the gifts of the spirit', (prophecy, healing, all knowledge).

Finally, Transpersonal Psychology does not (as in some movements) seek merely to transcend. Escape, kicks, fun, it surely can be and often is (from our troubled world) but not tripping for tripping's sake. It is vigorously more, being psycho-spiritually an area for dynamic growth, enrichment and understanding. Deep quantum paradigms, so to speak, are outposted, highlighting all in spiritual overview, holistically, beyond linear causality and three dimensional space-time philosophy. As love, awareness, relativity of all things, inspire us, we cannot ourselves remain unloved, unevolved.

Background:

Stuart is himself both psychic and psychotherapist, after years in spiritual lay movements, yoga and eastern disciplines, hypnotherapy, running psycho-therapeutic communities and groups, after disillusionment with psychiatric attendant work in a then unenlightened system. As psychic studies became acceptable academic honours were then taken. Majoring in counselling, psychology and parapsychology, research and theses were in 'Paranormal Aspects of Psychotherapy' and 'Biofeedback in Altered States of Consciousness' (Stuart induced these in subjects by laying on of hands). Author of book

'Ghosts, ESP & Psychology' (My true experiences UK, NZ & Australia) retained to bring up to date recent personal growth in Reichan body-work, Gestalt, Primal therapy and principally Psychodrama (at which Stuart is a Role-trainer Directing of groups). Before leaving the United Kingdom, he founded the Parapsychological Spiritual Institute. Earlier accepted for membership of American and British Psychological Societies and Transpersonal Psychology memberships, etc.

Footnote:

This is a copy of a current brochure showing my rationale. The Psycho-Spiritual work ranges from every day Psychological Counselling to Altered States, Healing and ESP but nothing is new and St. Paul said most if not all of it in Corinthians, 1.12, 2000 years ago.

SAMPLE:
THE 'CHRISTOS', 'GEMINI' AND OTHER TECHNIQUES –
A WORKSHOP

A key to Altered States of Consciousness ('Past Lives', Rebirthing, Transpersonal Experiences).

At: Blue Mountains Private Clinic.

Workshop Director: Stuart Rolls Ph. D. (Psychology, Parapsychology, Transpersonal Psychology)

Rationale:

Maslow, Grof and others, in the wake of a more humanistic psychology, TM and the psychedelic revolution, examined non-narcotic ways of 'tripping' safely and more predictably beyond the paradigms of three dimensional space and time as we know it. Thus from transhumanistic was born transpersonal psychology. The rationale was to recognise certain 'highs', 'peaks', spiritual or mystical states as not necessarily psychoses etc., to be conventionally (non-spiritually) pathologised. From many ASCs (altered states of consciousness) humankind gets an overview or souls-view that positively helps integrate emotional, physical, intellectual as well as spiritual experiences as a whole.

The safe 'waking-dream' like state is reached by easy relaxation, guided imagery, visualisation and energy balancing etc., sometimes with music. It is not recommended as a party game as amateurs could leave subjects hazy, denying them therapeutic integration.

Therapist's Role:

Stuart's perceived role is that of 'bridge-builder' between lay movements and establishment psychology. As a Role Trainer in Psychodrama directorship he utilises and expands its methodology uniquely. This empowers people to get the best out of their transpersonal/parapsychological work.

Therapist's Background:

Has included psychiatric and care work, hypnotherapy, psychical research and personal development in ESP, healing and yoga etc. He holds a BA (Arts/Social Science) through Philosophy and Psychology to a separate BA (Honours). MA/PhD programme (Counselling, Psychology and Para-psychology).

Diploma in Parapsychology. Doctoral thesis 'Paranormal Aspects of Psychotherapy', book pending 'Ghosts, ESP & Psychology' (My true Experiences UK, NZ & Australia).

POETRY

Karma Drama

Karma guides us through many experiential lives,
Reincarnated again from Heaven's eternal skies,
Our soul-needs all recorded in afterlife archives,
Life's schoolroom lessons beckoning – no surprise!

Where to next, we tremulously seek to enquire?
We've lived elsewhere and learned so materially,
In what better lives might we more have aspired?
Hoping above hope we'd grown ever spiritually!

Live peacefully now whilst reviewing life's dues,
Keep Karma's fair and just dramas ever in view,
Earths spiritual therapies, we may hold in purview,
Enlightening past conflict with new things to do.

Earth's old negatives then hold no tenure or lease,
To the schoolroom of life we can evermore be true,
The best of life still helps us to transcendent peace,
An everlasting legacy; soul-right not just for the few.

by Stuart R Rolls

Yoga Girl in Lotus Posture

Enigmatic smile in bliss of meditation,
Beatific beauty, where gone in elation?
For some considerable while in dedication,
Where and how far, not just for her nation?

In blessed feeling, she loves the 'All',
Beyond creation yet within its call,
Sanctifying the whole within its recall,
That she might help others lest they fall.

To know the dedication of Eternity,
To give of herself so bountifully,
Well might she one day exalted be,
Earth Mother's sweet young prodigy.

by Stuart R Rolls

Oneness and Source

We're All within the Oneness
Eternal patterns to read,
As Universes seemingly evolve
And all within makes progress.

The 'Seers' see this unfoldment
Even to our very selves,
As repeat incarnations raise us
To spirit heights as yet untold.

No beginning and no end,
Is all in constant flux?
One source or is it many
That we barely comprehend?

The same for Worlds and States
Self centred in stuck beliefs;
Do realise compromise and sharing
Reveal all that Oneness indicates.

All is cyclical, some do suggest,
Source reminiscent of its parts,
Allows contention to help all see
Peaceful journeying through Eternity.

by Stuart R Rolls

Dream's Dream

Dream announces 'I am' from the All,
A timespent birth differentiated into me,
Earthly dimensions paying one more call,
Then back to that higher, true reality.

Not that it's lesser, where no us to recall,
Or the dream transformed of human identity,
No more of you and me; oh! fates befall,
Though evermore of us in All, endlessly.

Oh! Where were we all before 'the fall'
Completely risen beyond reach of infinity?
Where we were not so infinitely small,
But blissfully one everlasting creativity?

The dream enlightened me to see,
That all's not lost, collectively,
Where we Godlike see ourselves, yet oversee,
As One, all others—all things, in Eternity.

Being the One dream, creates all dreams,
All Worlds, space, ebb, flow, constancy,
Bliss forever, everything, all of these themes,
Dream dreaming dreams that also dream thee!

by Stuart R Rolls

Meditation

Tidy all unruly thoughts; sense them as they truly are,
Seen as strays upon a catwalk, that do not wander far,
Let them strut and model, change to many a different guise,
Then you'll be aware of them, and there'll be no surprise.

Transform them, clear the stage, other things come into view,
Holisms, feelings, different pictures, will telepath to you,
Helpers who've gone before, knock upon your psychic door,
Open up, let them in, with spiritual gifts that help you soar,

Out there with the stars and cosmos, the paranormal best,
All transpersonal knowledge for your shining inner quest,
You too can beam and prophecy, see 'Eternity in an hour',
Pass right through mortality, yet hold 'infinity's flower'.

by Stuart R Rolls

Ode to Mounts and Vales

I live you softly, in all that which silken touch incites,
Observe your beauteous forms in life's sensual way,
Hear love's longing from all your climaxing heights,
Carnally knowing, yet in your ineffably set Eternity.

Abreast your softened shapes all is touchingly aright,
Iced caps melt streams of awestruck tears to convey
To pristine folds, below thrust mountains upward fight,
'Love's pierced innocence mounts with our mortal clay'.

Eternal motion too, as lifts our wings, lets them alight,
Down safely on time's sand, as tempest and storm allay
Themselves, to show all of flowering Nature is not might,
Nor all Eternity, that balances our yin and yang in sway.

Within the All I know long intimate stillness of the night,
Yet fondling too, the sure climax of the shortest day,
Beyond which the stars still undress their naked light,
Shown teasingly there, in amorous, orgiastic display.

In Oneness all seasons appear; ever circle round in flight,
As loved faces of the one blissful love in which we lay
Ourselves down in everlasting passion, past mortal sight,
No matter how Worldly desiring we love, learn and pray.

Sacred Creation of all our Divine loving, still be us finite,
Yet as Source, Love Universal, lovemaking in as we may,
With mating, caressing, orgasmic, fecund, union Infinite;
Oh! Harmony of ecstasy, in you, we do but dance and play.

by Stuart R Rolls

From Auguries of Innocence

To see a world in a grain of sand
And a Heaven in a Wild flower,
Hold Infinity in the palm of your hand,
And Eternity in an hour.

William Blake

***

'In my beginning is my end'

T.S. Elliot

***

ANONYMOUS QUOTATION

*Whole mind techniques communicate extraordinarily
with sub-conscious mind and psychic faculty,
transforming restricting data along the way,
to Eternity, no less. (the Author)*

Alarming epidemic on the increase

Be on the lookout for symptoms of inner peace. The hearts of a great many have already been exposed to it. People everywhere could come down with it in epidemic proportions. This could pose a serious threat to what has been a fairly stable condition of conflict in the World!

Some signs and symptoms of inner peace:

- A tendency to think and act spontaneously rather than on fears based on past experiences.

- An unmistakable ability to enjoy each moment.

- A loss of interest in judging other people.

- A loss of interest in judging self.

- A loss of interest in interpreting the actions of others.

- A loss of interest in conflict.

- A loss of the ability to worry.

- Frequent overwhelming episodes of appreciation

- Frequent attacks of smiling.

- An increasing tendency to let things happen rather than make them happen.

- An increased susceptibility to the love extended by others as well as the uncontrollable urge to extend it.

- A tendency to think and act paranormally!

Warning

If you have some or all of the above symptoms, please be advised that your condition of inner peace may be so far advanced as to be incurable. If you are exposed to anyone exhibiting any of these symptoms, remain so only at your own risk.

Anon.

NEWS ARTICLES

Excerpts from author's lawyer friend's website; see *Victor Zammit* under Author's Recommended Readings and in Web Page.

THE US GOVERNMENT ACKNOWLEDGES PSYCHIC POWER IS REAL

Perhaps those ignorant, highly negatively entrenched closed minded skeptics who keep repeating 'there is no such thing as psychic phenomena' can explain why a psychic was awarded the Legion of Merit for psychic services. This award is the second highest award that the US Army can make during peace time. It was given to remote viewer Joe McMoneagle, with the approval of US Congress, for his brilliant psychic work. The citation reads:

> *"While with his command, he used his talents and expertise in the execution of more than 200 missions, addressing over 150 essential elements of information. These EEI contained critical intelligence reported at the highest echelons of our military and government, including such national level agencies as the Joint Chiefs of Staff, DIA, NSA, CIA, DEA, and the Secret Service, producing crucial and vital intelligence unavailable from any other source."*

THE OBJECTIVE EVIDENCE FOR THE AFTERLIFE HAS NOTHING TO DO WITH RELIGION OR PERSONAL BELIEF!

On Victor Zammit's site you will get to know the findings of many of highly intelligent scientists, empiricists and other professionals who systematically investigated the afterlife and psychic phenomena over more than a century. AND you will get to know with *absolute certainty* that everyone survives death. The afterlife is inevitable and has huge consequences.

No genius scientist, no genius skeptic, no genius materialist has been able to disprove the afterlife evidence.

Many scientists who investigated the afterlife evidence now accept the afterlife – see below:

Do you know exactly what is going to happen to you when you pass on?

FINANCIALLY AND MORALLY SUPPORTED BY THE CHINESE GOVERNMENT – THE 'SUPER PSYCHICS':

"The 'Super Psychics' of China, have been recognised and nurtured by their Government for the last 25 years. Paul Dong and Thomas E Raffill, authors of China's Super Psychics, state that millions of dollars have been spent researching EHF, or 'Extra Human Function' in these children. Schools and research centres are widespread throughout the country. By 1997, 1000,000 of these Children has been recognised. "… As I said before, whoever masters the paranormal, will master the world, no doubt about that."

Reincarnation
is
coming back!

MEDITATIONAL DATA

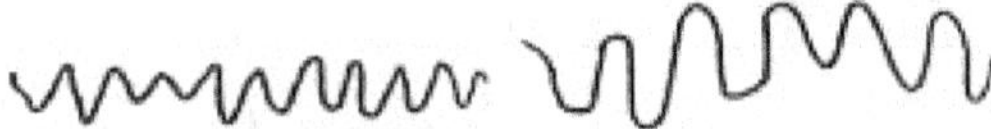

It should help readers to think of beta brain waves as scrunched up, highly alert, active, busy at tasks, even 'hyped' or intense:

Alpha into theta as stretching out more; relaxing one in say creative flow—don't go too'far out' if driving or busy with machinery etc! Blends of all above, fine in martial art etc or calm and sure activity; illumination as in meditative therapy:

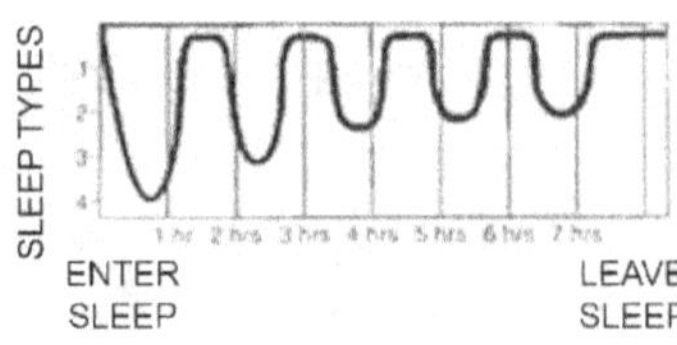

Theta/delta progress unto sleep, paranormality, deeper enlightenment, transcendence etc if entrained 'blending-waves' hold back sleep; see book.

WHOLE BRAIN SYNCHRONY, creates best results of course, requiring that both sides of brain, left and right, match up, after meditational entrainment, best served by specialised tapes, as detailed in the book. One will find graphs showing 'twin brain' print-outs in specialised books.

REM SLEEP DATA (AVERAGE 5 REM PEAKS NIGHTLY)

DREAMOLOGY CHART

USEFUL ADDRESSES

The Journal of Transpersonal Psychology
Sofia University
(formerly Institute of Transpersonal Psychology)
1069 East Meadow Circle
Palo Alto, CA 94303, United States

Spiritual Gazette
Spiritualist Association of Great Britain
11 Belgrave Road
London SW1V 1RB

The Christian Parapsychologist
The Churches Fellowship for Psychical and Spiritual Studies
Rural Workshop
South Road
North Somercotes
Lincolnshire, LN11 7PZ

The Society for Psychical Research (prints journals)
49 Marloes Road
Kensington
London, W8 6LA

Psychic News
Suite 6, Thremhall Park
Start Hill, Bishops Stortford
Hertfordshire CM22 7WE

Two Worlds
PO Box 55307
London, SE16 6WW

The Healing Trust
(formerly The National Federation of Spiritual Healers)
21 York Road
Northampton, NN1 5QG

CONTACT THE AUTHOR

C/– MoshPit Publishing
PO Box 147
Hazelbrook NSW 2779
Australia

Or via:
www.moshpitpublishing.com.au

DISCLAIMER

This series of books is advisory. Any health problems that could be affected by high tech. in meditational or dreamwork should be the responsibility of the individual; related choices should be made in consultation with one's own medical advisers.

BIBLIOGRAPHY

1. Beloff, John: New Dimensions in Parapsychology

2. Church of England *Report on Spiritualism* (headed by Archbishop Lang 1937)

3. Bhaktivedanta Swami Prabhupada. A.C.: *Easy Journey to Other Planets*

4. Betjeman, Sir John (British Poet Laureate) in Skelton, R. (edition): *Poetry of the Thirties*

5. Stevenson, Dr Ian: cases of reincarnation, several publications

6. Moody, Raymond A.: *Reflections on Life After Life*

7. Grof, Stanislav: *LSD Psychotherapy* and other titles

8. Moreno, J.L.: *Who Shall Survive?*

9. Perls, Fritz: *Gestalt Therapy Verbatim*

10. Manning, Matthew: *The Link*

11. Roll, W.G.: *The Poltergeist*

12. Guirdham, Arthur: *Paradise Found, Reflections on Psychic Survival*

13. West, Morris: *The Heretic* (book and play)

14. Nostradamus: *Centuries* – many books published about his original work.

15. Ferguson, Marilyn: *The Aquarian Conspiracy*

16. Swedenborg, Emanuel: *Heaven and Hell* (Swedenborg Foundation)

17. Weed, Joseph J.: *Wisdom of the Mystic Masters*

18. Yogananda, Paramhansa: *Autobiography of a Yogi*

19. Zammit, Victor: *A lawyer presents the case for the afterlife: irrefutable objective evidence*

20. See Web Page at back for Victor's regular Friday Reports detail: www.victorzammit.com

AUTHOR'S RECOMMENDED READINGS

Stuart especially recommends the following books AND readings for much of the miraculous same:

1. Weed, Joseph J: *Wisdom of the Mystic Masters*, Parker Publishing, February 1971 ISBN: 978-0139615320

2. Swedenborg, Emanuel: (1688–1772), *Heaven and Hell*, Swedenborg Foundation, http://www.swedenborg.com/

3. Zammit, Victor: *A Lawyer Presents the Case for the Afterlife*, ISBN: 095-8011508 © 2006 Gammell Pty Ltd, PO Box 1810, Dee Why, NSW, Australia 2099.

WEB PAGE

DAVID THOMPSON, materialisation medium
http://www.davidthompson.com.au

VICTOR ZAMMIT
http://www.victorzammit.com

Victor's website puts out a worldwide 'Friday Report' with his wife, Wendy. They famously cover every aspect of things psychic and psycho-spiritual, as in my book writings along the whole spectrum. As friends we've worked with World class top materialisation medium David (as above). You can subscribe to both these websites online.

Victor and Wendy's other sites:
http://www.facebook.com/afterlifeevidence
https://twitter.com/AfterlifeEv

Victor's veracity at working with David, myself often present, has his (Victor's) stamp of having worked in the High Court of Australia (solicitor/attorney), also the Supreme Court of NSW. He was attracted too by the humanitarian inter-faiths of such as the Wayside Chapel and its social justice, in doing good for all humanity, not particular religions etc. who better to evidence the afterlife for all of us born on Earth? (Wendy too!)

Together we have witnessed David Thompson strapped securely with seals in a wooden armchair raised to séance room ceilings, whilst his guides from spirit and séance members departed loved ones etc., talk through him. At other times, David, aroused from sleepy stages by his guide/s, outstandingly joins in conversations with them. All this with his creaky wooden armchair – ties holding him in, still up, so to speak, on the ceiling (ties still secure upon séance close down).

David is a wonderfully accurate clairvoyant, too (evidence in my early books). I don't know if he's been conscious of bi-location (being in and seen in two places at once, as I, a certain Monsignor and a Tibetan mystic, Chapter 3, have). This could explain why some at David's séances think he's left his shackled seat.

www.ingramcontent.com/pod-product-compliance
Lightning Source LLC
Chambersburg PA
CBHW070810240726
48654CB00007B/283